THE MIRACLE PLAY IN ENGLAND.

LOST SOULS.

*(From a Fresco of " The Day of Judgment" in the Chapel of Holy Cross,
Stratford-on-Avon.*

The Miracle Play

in England, . . .

An Account of the Early Religious Drama,

By Sidney W. Clarke.

"At Pentecost,
When all our pageants of delight were play'd."
—*Two Gentlemen of Verona, Act iv., Scene 4.*

HASKELL HOUSE
Publishers of Scholarly Books
NEW YORK
1964

published by

HASKELL HOUSE

Publishers of Scholarly Books

30 East 10th Street • New York, N. Y. 10003

Library of Congress Catalog Card Number: 65-15874

PRINTED IN UNITED STATES OF AMERICA

𝔓reface.

I HAVE attempted in these pages to trace concisely, and I hope intelligibly, the gradual growth of the religious drama in this country, where, from a date somewhat subsequent to the Conquest to the time of the Reformation, it occupied a place in public estimation and favour little, if at all, inferior to that now held by the secular stage.

While not altogether neglecting the literary and dramatic features of the Miracle Plays, it has rather been my endeavour to give an account of the manner in which the people at large entered into the spirit of the performances, and to tell how they presented and embellished their plays.

If I succeed in conveying to those who read these pages some idea of what these Miracle Plays really were in matter and in representation, and in thereby indicating the extent to which they influenced the life of the people, in which they were so great an element, I shall be content.

SIDNEY W. CLARKE.

LAMB BUILDING,
    TEMPLE.

List of References.

Wright's " Early Mysteries."

Collier's " History of English Dramatic Poetry."

Ward's " History of English Dramatic Literature " *(Macmillan)*.

Symond's " Shakespeare's Predecessors in the English Drama " *(Smith, Elder & Co.)*.

Pollard's " English Miracle Plays " *(Clarendon Press)*.

Sharp's " Dissertation on the Coventry Mysteries."

Miss Toulmin Smith's " York Plays " *(Clarendon Press)*.

" Coventry Mysteries " *(Shakespeare Society)*.

" Chester Plays " *(Shakespeare Society)*.

" Towneley Mysteries " *(Surtees Society)*.

And other works mentioned in the text.

Contents.

The Miracle Play in England.

CHAPTER I.

The Origin of Drama.

THERE is no better established fact in the whole history of intellectual progress than that the dramas of the world, both ancient and modern, have originated in the religious observances of the people among whom they existed. The ancient Greek drama, the earliest of which we have any knowledge, furnishes an excellent example of this great truth ; for it was not only evolved out of the wild and furious dance to Bacchus, but all through its periods of development and of greatest excellence it never entirely lost its connection with the religious ceremonial of the nation. Dionysus, God of Life and Death, God of the Fertile Earth, God of Wine, was the father alike of Greek tragedy and comedy. Drama formed a part of his worship, and the theatre was the temple in which he was enthroned in the person of his two daughters, twin representatives of his Janus-like character, and of the double aspect of life. The production of a play was a religious function, and in the large stone shrine of Dionysus at Athens the entire population were wont to assemble, to celebrate in honour of the god, from dawn to dark, on the occasion of the performance of the new pieces. Every citizen was entitled, as of right, to attend, and even when a charge began to be made

1

for admission, if the sum charged was beyond the means of
any citizen he had only to apply to the magistrates, who
were bound to supply him from the public funds with the
necessary oboli.   In the middle of the orchestra, which
occupied the floor of the house, stood the altar, on which a
sacrifice was offered before the performance commenced,
and round which the chorus was grouped.   In the best seat
sat the priest of Dionysus, presiding over the festival of his
god, and the god himself was supposed to be present.   In
the evening, before the dramatic displays began, the statue
of the god was taken out of its shrine, carried in a procession
by torchlight to the theatre, and placed in the orchestra in
full view of the stage, and there it remained until the close
of the festival.   The festivals were not held at the will of
man, but were established in obedience to the commands of
the oracle, and the plays, or at least some of them, were
supposed to have been written at the inspiration of the
divinity.   During the festivals the whole city gave itself up
to pleasure and to worship.   Peace and harmony were
presumed to prevail; distraints for debt was forbidden by
law during their continuance; prisoners were temporarily
released from gaol to enable them to join in the worship;
anyone committing an assault received a specially severe
punishment, as being guilty of an outrage against religion.
To preserve the sacredness of the performance no person
suffering from civil disability was allowed to take part in a
chorus.   Any form of insult committed in the theatre was
punished with death as sacrilege; while the persons of the
poets, actors, singers, and dancers were regarded as sacred
for the time being.   In short, the performance of the old
Greek drama was essentially part of a religious celebration,

and was intended not merely as an amusement for the people but as an act of homage and reverence to the god. *

The Indian drama, like the Greek, owed its origin to a union of song and dance at the festivals of the gods, and was in its prime only performed on solemn occasions of a public nature, and at seasons sacred to some divinity. The germ of Chinese drama was the sacred or symbolical dance, and in Japan theatrical performances were evolved out of a dance called the "Sambôso," which was performed as a charm against volcanic eruptions.

The Roman drama was not of native or independent origin, but was an offshoot of Greek drama, and was, if tradition supported by Livy and Valerius Maximus may be trusted, introduced into Rome in order to appease the wrath of the gods at a time of pestilence. In like manner, when we come to investigate the origin of modern drama, we shall find that origin to be in religious worship, and that, as in ancient Greece so in mediæval Europe, religion gave birth to drama. But first let us see why drama had to be born again.

Under the later Roman Empire drama, reflecting the manners and morals of the people, reached such a state of vicious degredation that it became an abomination. The theatre was overshadowed by the attractions of the amphi-theatre and the circus, and in its endeavour to compete with these rivals it fell to gross buffoonery and open obscenity. The Christian Church, finding reformation hopeless, placed drama under its severest condemnation, and when Christianity became the acknowledged religion of the Empire the doom of the theatre was sealed.

* See Haigh's "Attic Theatre," chapter I, section I.

The doctrine of suppression extended from the drama to all kinds of profane learning, with the result that all art and culture became extinct, except perhaps in the monasteries, and the lay world wallowed for centuries in a slough of ignorance and prejudice.

From the fourth to the tenth centuries profane art in all its branches was practically non-existant. A few Latin plays formed on the classic model, but dealing with religious subjects, were produced in the monasteries, but merely as literary exercises. The suppression by the Church of its pet abomination the theatre was effectual and complete.

Although the Church for its own purpose had suppressed drama, it is a curious commentary on the futility of human endeavour that the Church for its own purpose was obliged to resurrect what it had suppressed. Little as it may now bear traces of its origin, the theatre of Europe, and more particularly the theatre of England, is the offspring of religious worship. Its cradle was upon the steps of the altar, and in the years of its struggling infancy it was nurtured by ecclesiasticism and fostered by clerical care.

The form that this early drama took was that which we know as the Mystery or the Miracle Play. The very name shows the ecclesiastical origin, as the word mystery is but the French *mystère*, derived from *ministère*, because the clergy, the *ministerium*, or *ministri Ecclesiae*, were the first actors.

Though the names "Mystery" and "Miracle Play" are generally used indiscriminately to denote a religious play, each has a distinct technical meaning. Strictly, Miracle Plays are those dealing with incidents in the lives of saints and martyrs; while Mysteries are concerned with the

Scriptural narrative only, prominence being given to the story of man's fall and redemption. In England the term Miracle Play was given to any kind of sacred play.

The cradle of English drama rested on the altar. The old ritual of the church bristled with the germs of drama, and those germs were developed and expanded mainly on account of Latin, an unknown tongue to the masses of the people, being the language used in the churches. The Bible was a sealed book to the laity, and even if it had been free and open few could read. The clergy thus found it necessary to devise some means of explaining and bringing home the meaning of the ritual, and of teaching the truths of doctrine and Holy Writ to an unlettered and ignorant people. In addition to preaching the truths they had to proclaim they acted them, and in its early state the miracle play is nothing more than an acted sermon. Let us take an example of the crudest form of the miracle play. It would be more properly described as a series of living pictures than as a play, and was probably performed almost entirely in dumb show. Imagine a church dedicated to St. Nicholas. On that Saint's day the clergy of the church would desire to demonstrate to the congregation the virtues of their patron saint. This is how they did it :—The image of the saint was removed from its shrine, and a priest, dressed to represent the image, took its place. The service of the day commences, and at a suitable moment a pause is made for the representation of the miracle ; then another priest, dressed as a rich heathen, comes in at the church door and advances to the shrine, where he deposits his treasure, and calls on the saint to guard it for him while he goes away on a journey. As soon as the heathen has gone robbers enter the church, then stealthily creep up to the shrine, and silently carry off the treasure.   Soon the heathen returns ; on finding his property has been stolen he flies into a rage, and upbraids and beats the image of the saint which had failed to protect his treasure.   But upon this the image moves, descends from its niche, goes out and reasons with the robbers, and forces them to make restitution.   Terrified by the miracle the thieves return trembling up the church, and bring back all they had taken.   The saint's image returns to its niche. The heathen is transported with joy ; he sings and adores the image.   At this point another priest, personating the saint himself, appears on the scene, and bids the heathen worship God alone—the heathen thereupon proclaims his conversion to the true faith, and the church service is again proceeded with.

This in substance is one of the earliest English Miracle Plays of which we have any knowledge.   By degrees this crude form was elaborated, music and singing were pressed into service, until at length we get more advanced towards true drama in such episodes as the Offices of Easter and the Shepherds.   The former was performed in churches at Easter time to illustrate to the people the story of the Resurrection.   At the appointed place in the Easter service, three priests, representing the three Maries, slowly advanced up the church to where a grave had been prepared.   An angel sitting by the side of the grave asks them whom they seek, and the women reply that they seek for Jesus of Nazareth the crucified.   The dialogue and action then follow the gospel story, till finally a priest personating the Saviour appears and announces His Resurrection. This is the signal for the choir to join in with a joyous

Alleluia, and the play ends with the singing of the *Te Deum.*

The Office of the Shepherds was solemnized or performed on Christmas eve. A cradle was placed on the altar, and beside it an image of the Virgin Mary. A number of the clergy represented the shepherds, carrying crooks and having with them real sheep and dogs. Some of the shepherds feign to sleep, some to watch their flocks, when suddenly all are aroused as a sweet-voiced choir boy, dressed as an angel, mounts the pulpit, and from there, after a blast from the trumpeters, announces the birth of Jesus. Thereupon a number of singing boys posted in the galleries in the clere-story, and representing the multitude of the heavenly host, begin to sing "Glory to God in the Highest and on earth peace, goodwill toward men."

The shepherds proceed up the church to the manger, where other priests, personating the midwives, show the child Jesus and bid them proclaim His birth to the people. The shepherds adore the child and His mother, and then march through the church singing a hymn of praise.

It has been generally supposed that up to this point the characters in these church representations were acted solely by the clergy and the members of the church choirs, but it is probable that in some cases laymen took part in the performances. For instance, it is unlikely that in remote towns and villages the clerical staff of a church would be sufficient in number to perform such episodes as those we have just considered, and in an old Dutch novel probably dating from the end of the 15th century, a translation of which is printed in Garrick's "Old Plays," there is a story that certainly corroborates this theory of the employment of

laymen as actors. The book is entitled "A merye Jest of a
man that was called Howleglas," in the original Dutch he is
named *Ulenspiegle*, and is an account of the adventures of a
rogue of that name. In the course of the story we are told
how Howleglas goes to live in the house of a priest who
makes him his parish clerk. The priest is not a credit to
his cloth for he keeps a mistress. Howleglas and this
woman quarrel, and the rogue determines to be revenged on
her for the offence she has given him. His opportunity
comes at Easter, when it was the custom to play the
Resurrection of our Lord in the church. On this occasion,
so the story proceeds, "because than the men wer not
learned, nor could not read, the priest toke his leman, and
put her in the grave for an aungell: and this seing
Howleglas, toke to hym iij of the symplest persons that were
in the towne, that played the iij Maries; and the parson
played Christe, with a baner in his hand. Than saide
Howleglas to the symple persons, Whan the aungel asketh
you whome you seke, you may saye, The parsons leman with
one iye. Than it fortuned that the tyme was come that they
must playe, and the aungel asked them whom they sought,
and than sayd they, as Howleglas had shewed and lerned
them afore, and than answered they, We seke the priests
leman with one iye. And than the prieste might heare that
he was mocked. And whan the priestes leman herd that,
she arose out of the grave, and would have smyten with her
fist Howleglas upon the cheke, but she missed him and
smote one of the simple persons that play one of the thre
Maries; and he gave her another; and then toke she him
by the heare; and that seing his wyfe came running hastely
to smite the priestes leaman; and than the priest seeing this

caste down hys baner and went to helpe his woman, so that the one gave the other sore strokes, and made great noyse in the churche. And than Howleglas seyng them lyinge together by the eares in the bodi of the churche, went his way out of the village, and came no more there."

It was to the stage of naïve dramatization exemplified by these Offices of Easter and the Shepherds that the latent dramatic elements of church ceremonial had been developed on the Continent about the time of the Norman Conquest. We have now to see how in England the miracle play reached its greatest effectiveness and its highest state of development.

CHAPTER II.

The Beginnings of English Drama.

IT was about the middle of the seventh century that literature had first ventured to raise its head in England, and up to the coming of the Normans it maintained a somewhat precarious existence—confined to metrical paraphrases of the Bible, war songs chronicles of the valorous deeds of kings and warriors, translations from the Latin, but never a trace of drama. The puny growth was cut short, almost annihilated, by the shock of the Conquest, and for a hundred or a hundred-and-fifty years English literature almost ceased to exist. It was to the church of the day that it owed its revivication, and the form the renewed life took was the dramatic.

The alien clergy who flocked over in the train of the Conqueror brought with them the germ of the miracle play— the liturgical mystery—and they speedily made use of their ornate ritual, dumb shows, and processions, to attract their new congregations, and to impress on them the knowledge of scriptural truths.

Out of the ordinary service of the church they evolved spectacular effect, action, and dialogue, the three elements of drama, and gradually the representations interpolated into the services were elaborated into true dramatic form. The dialogue at first was in Latin—the language of the church,— and since that was an unknown tongue to the masses of the people the required effect was produced almost entirely by the acting. The next stage was reached when French or Anglo-Norman became the medium of expression, and at last, about the thirteenth century, the great plunge was taken, and English, the language of the common people, was used. Immediately, the religious drama bounded into popularity. The wandering minstrels, jongleurs, story-tellers, and other popular entertainers saw its great possibilities, and began to amuse the people in the streets and open places, on holidays and at fairs, with acted scenes from the Bible story or the legends of the saints. These holidays and fairs clashing with the holy days and festivals of the church, the clergy found the people unwilling to come to service, preferring the amusing performances outside to the duller though more reverent representations in the sacred buildings. The clergy in this emergency acted with a promptitude and determination that did them credit. They excommunicated all these poachers on their preserves, and themselves started full and complete performances in the churches. The result was electrical—the churches soon proved quite inadequate to accommodate the vast crowds that flocked to see the miracle plays, and, for the convenience of both actors and audience, the venue was changed from the altar to the porch, thence for a similar reason to the churchyard, and finally the sacred precincts were abandoned for the public streets and open spaces about the town. Every foot that increased the distance of the place of performance from the church weakened the ability of the clergy to retain the performances in their own hands. Once the plays were removed from the church the members of the city companies and the trade-guilds aspired to be actors, while the wandering minstrels were ready to lend their aid. As the performances became dissevered from the services of the church, the lay actors began to introduce the comic element, and to multiply the characters. Though the clergy withdrew to some extent from participation in the performance of miracle plays as the lay actors came more and more to the front, it must not be supposed that the clergy altogether ceased to act, or that no further representations took place in the churches. In fact, we find that for many years the clerical and lay performances went on side by side, in spite of a growing feeling that the clergy should not act and that the churches were hardly the proper places for performances in which scenes of buffoonery began to intermingle with the simple scripture narrative. In 1210 a papal edict forbade the clergy to act in churches or at mummings, a prohibition which was repeated by the Council of Trèves in 1227.

Acting in the churches did not altogether cease, however, for about 1300 we find that a compromise had been made —the clergy were allowed to represent the Resurrection and the Nativity in the churches, but were not to act in any open places. Still later we find lay actors performing in churches; thus in the accounts of S. Mary's, Leicester, under the year 1491 is the item—

"Paid to the players on New Year's Day at Even in the church—6d."

and in 1499 2s. was paid for a like purpose. At Bewdley, in 1572, we find that 6s. 8d. was paid to the queen's players for performing in the church. In 1542 Bonner, Bishop of London, issued a proclamation to the clergy of his diocese forbidding all manner of common plays, games, or interludes to be played, set forth, or declared within the churches or chapels. Such prohibitions as this were probably not very efficacious, for in "The Third Blast of Retreat from Plaies," published in 1580, there is a complaint that the players were permitted "to publish their mamettrie in everie temple of God, and that throughout England." But in 1589 an injunction was ratified in Rome prohibiting all the clergy from playing in Miracle Plays, and the canons of James I., promulgated in 1603, forbade any play to be performed in a church.

A curious reference to these semi-dramatic representations in English churches occurs in Lambarde's "Topographical Dictionary," which was probably written about 1570-1580. The author, after stating that at Witney in Kent the clergy used to set forth yearly, in the manner of a show or interlude, the Resurrection of our Lord, goes on to say that "the more lyvely heareby to exhibite to the eye the hole action of the resurrection, the priestes garnished out certain smalle puppettes, representing the persons of Christe, the Watchmen, Marie, and others." He also states that he had as a child been present in St. Paul's Cathedral in London, at Whitsuntide when "the comyne downe of the Holy Ghoste was set forthe by a white pigion that was let to fly out of a hole that yet is to be sene in the mydst of the roofe of the greate ile, and by a longe censer which, descendinge out of the same place almost to the verie grounde, was swinged up and downe . . . breathinge out over the whole churche and companie a most pleasant perfume of suche swete thinges as burned therein. With the like doome shewes also they used everie where to furnish sondrye parts of their church service as by their spectacles of the Nativitie, Passion, and Assension."

This custom is also referred to in the following lines from Barnaby Googe's translation of "Naogeorgus":—

" On Whit-Sunday white pigeons tame in strings from heaven flie,
　And one that framed is of wood still hangeth in the skie.
　Thou seest how they with idols play, and teach the people too ;
　None otherwise than little girls with puppets used to do."

The first Miracle Play known to have been acted in
England was the Miracle Play of S. Catherine, mentioned
by Matthew Paris as having been represented at Dunstable
about the year 1100.　It was the work of one Geoffrey, a
schoolmaster of that town, and was performed by his pupils,
the costumes being borrowed from the Abbey at S. Albans.
On the first night of the performance Geoffrey's house was
burnt down, and the wardrobe (including the costly
borrowed vestments), the properties, and the books were
entirely consumed.　Geoffrey evidently looked upon this
disaster as a judgment upon him for his sin in writing a play,
and for his greater sin in training children as actors, and
thus giving them a liking for what some " unco' guid " folks
term the " Devil's Profession."　At any rate, he turned
monk, and, repenting of the errors of his former life, in due
time became abbot of the abbey whose vestments he had
lost.　William Stephanides, or Fitz-Stephen, a monk of
Canterbury in the reign of Henry II., wrote " An account of
the most noble City of London," in which occurs the first
mention we have of dramatic entertainments in England
(Matthew Paris not writing till half a century later), as
follows :—" London, instead of common interludes belonging to the theatres, has plays of a more holy subject—
representation of those miracles which the holy confessors
wrought, or of the sufferings wherein the glorious constancy
of the martyrs did appear."　Stephanides also describes the
performance of a Miracle Play founded on incidents in the

life of S. Thomas à Beckett, and says that such entertainments had then been long common in England.

By the end of the 13th century the representation of the miracle plays had passed almost entirely into the hands of the laity, and more especially of the great trade guilds, who began to give performances in honour of their patron saints, and under their direction we find the miracle play at its best. A great impetus was given to the activity of the guilds by a decree of the Council of Vienne in 1311 ordaining the strict observance of the feast of Corpus Christi on the Thursday after Trinity Sunday. This day was adopted by many of the trade guilds as their great annual festival, and as the day is generally one of the longest in the year, it lent itself to the production of an elaborate cycle of plays in which each craft could enact a separate scene. The simple miracle play was extended into a grand performance, which commenced with the Creation, covered most of the chief events in the Bible narrative, and ended with the Day of Judgment. Of these great cycles, four have come down to us as the important remains of English religious drama. The texts of the plays acted at York, Wakefield, Chester, and Coventry, are the only complete relics we possess of those great series of miracle plays which, between the years 1350 and 1500, were acted all over the country with the greatest possible success. Besides these great centres we know of miracle plays being acted at about thirty other places in England, and from some few of these fragments of the plays have been preserved.

CHAPTER III.

The York Plays.

BY far the most important and interesting of the four series or cycles of English miracle plays that have survived to the present day, are those that were performed in the streets of York, from the fourteenth to the sixteenth centuries, by the members of the craft and trade guilds, with the sanction, and under the active supervision, of the City Fathers. These plays are forty-eight in number, and were probably composed about the middle of the fourteenth century, though the manuscript that has been preserved does not appear to have been written till about 1430. This manuscript has an interesting history; we know that it was revised at the time of the Reformation, and it now consists of 270 leaves of parchment or vellum, of which forty-eight are blank, encased in an ancient wooden binding. The volume came into the possession of Horace Walpole in 1764 for the insignificant sum of one guinea, and was purchased on the dispersion of the Walpole collection by a bookseller named Rodd for £220 10s. od. From Rodd the book passed, in 1842, to Mr. Heywood Bright, of Bristol, who gave £235 for it, and only two years later it was sold to the Rev. Thomas Russell for £305. Finally, it became the property of the late Lord Ashburnham, and still forms a leading feature of the Ashburnham library. Though the manuscript gives the text of forty-eight plays, we know from

the records of the City of York that in the year 1415 there
were fifty-one plays acted, and at an earlier date as many as
fifty-seven; thus it is evident that several of the earlier plays
must either have been discontinued at the date of the
manuscript, or that the texts have been lost. It is well
known that wherever a long series of miracle plays was
performed the number of the plays was constantly changing.
Each trade guild was supposed to act a distinct play, and as
the guilds grew or declined in number and wealth, the cycle
had to be extended to make room for a new comer, or a play
had to be omitted because the craft to which it had been
allotted had ceased to exist, or had become too poor to be
able to bear the considerable charge of worthily presenting
its pageant.

Miracle plays seem to have been acted at York from a
very early date; the earliest notice we have of them is in
1378, but they had evidently been performed for many years
previously, while in 1394 we find them spoken of as having
existed for a very long time, and we know that in 1397
Richard II. was present at their performance.

The text of the plays is in the Northumbrian dialect, and
the metre is constantly varied to suit the subject matter of
the separate plays, while very creditable attempts are made
to fit the various characters with proper mediums of expression
—thus God, Abraham, and the Patriarchs express themselves
with becoming gravity and dignity; the diction of Jesus and
the Virgin Mary is simple and dignified; Satan, Pharoah,
Herod, Pilate, and Caiaphas are blusterous, pompous, and
daring. It is a noteworthy feature that in these plays even
those characters most calculated to arouse the clamorous
detestation of the audience are not wholly vicious—Pilate,

2

for instance, appears to be of a somewhat benevolent
disposition, and a rigid observer of justice; while even
Herod, always the villain of the piece in a miracle play, is
here shown as a sympathiser with those suffering under
unjust oppression.   The plays on the whole are reverent and
seemly in tone, are full of dramatic life and energy, and in
some plays, noteably those of the Passion and Crucifixion,
we find realism of a most impressive nature.   The subjects
extend from the Creation of the World, set out in the first of
the series, to Doomsday, which was illustrated in the final
pageant, and the text closely follows the Bible narrative, with
occasional excursions into the apocryphal legends of the day.
Now and then the author seizes the opportunity to urge some
point of doctrine or practice upon his audience, thus, in the
play of Cain and Abel, to emphasize the propriety of paying
tithes he makes an angel deliver a message from the Deity :—

> " The tente (1) to tyne (2) he askis, no more,
>   Of all the goodes he haves you sente, full trew. (3)
>   To offyr loke that ye be yore, (4)
>   And to my tale ye take entent, (5)
>   For ilke-a-lede (6) that liffe has tente, (7) shall you ensewe."(8)

A brief analysis of the plays composing the cycle is all
that can be attempted in these pages.   The first play deals
with the creation of the world and the fall of Lucifer.
The scene opens with God enthroned in Heaven :—

> " I am gracyus and grete, god withoutyn begynning,
>   I am maker unmade, all mighte es in me,
>   I am lyfe and way unto welth (9) wynnyng,
>   I am formaste and fyrste, als (10) I byd sall it be.
>   My blyssing of ble (11) sall be blendyng, (12)
>   And heldand (13) fro harme to be hydande, (14)

(1) Tenth part.   (2) Lose.   (3) Faith.   (4) Ready.   (5) Heed.   (6) Man.   (7) Given.
(8) Follow after.   (9) Salvation.   (10) As.   (11) Aspect.   (12) Blinding.   (13) Descending.   (14) Hiding.

> My body in blys ay abydande (1)
> Unedande (2) withoutyn any endyng."

God then creates the nine orders of angels, who sing a *Te deum*. Great dignity is conferred upon Lucifer, who assumes to himself the attributes of the Deity, and is punished by being thrown into Hell with those angels who worshipped him instead of God. The process of creation is then begun, and is continued in the second play. In the next man is made—

> " To keepe this worlde bothe more and lesse
> A skylfull beeste than will y make
> After my shappe and my likenesse,
> The whilke shalle wirshippe to me take."

Three plays are devoted to showing Adam and Eve in the Garden of Eden, their fall, and expulsion from Paradise. Then follows the story of Cain and Abel. An angel comes to the brothers, and bids them sacrifice a tenth part of their goods to God. Abel expresses his readiness to obey the Divine command, but Cain, with many imprecations, refuses to do so :—

> CAIN.—" We ! whythir now in wilde waneand, (3)
> Trowes thou I think to trusse (4) of towne ? (5)
> Goo, jape (6) thee, robard ungellande, (7)
> Me liste noyt nowe to rouk (8) nor rowne. (9)
>
> .   .   .   .   .   .
>
> Ya ! devell me thynketh that werke were waste
> That he no gaffe geffe hym agayne, to se.
> Now fekyll friendshippe for to fraste, (10)
> Me thynkith ther is in hym sarteyne.
> If he be moste in myghte and mayne,
>   What need has he ?"

There is a break here in the MS., and when it resumes,

---

(1) Abiding. (2) Unending. (3) Wilde waneand, query whether a form of swearing. (4) Prepare. (5) Farm. (6) Mock. (7) Quarrelsome thief. (8) Kneel. (9) Pray. (10) Prove.

Cain has evidently killed his brother, for an angel enters and asks—Where is Abel? Cain flies into a rage, strikes the angel, and is cursed.

Plays eight and nine have the building of the Ark and the Flood for their subjects. These plays, being performed by the Shipwrights' and Mariners' Guilds, are full of nautical touches—when Noah wants to find out whether the water is abating, he casts the lead in regular sailor fashion. Number ten represents the sacrifice of Isaac, and then there is a long jump to Pharoah and the bondage in Egypt. Pharoah boasts of his might, and orders the Israelites to be oppressed. The incident of Moses and the Burning Bush is represented, and then one after the other messengers come to tell Pharoah of the plagues that have fallen upon the land. He finally gives the Israelites leave to go, but pursues them to the Red Sea, where he and his men are drowned, while the Israelites raise a song of praise :—

> "Now ar we woune fra waa, and saved oute of the see,
> Cantemus domino, to god a sange syne wee."

The next play opens the New Testament series, and is prefaced by a prologue enumerating the prophecies of the Advent of Christ. An angel announces to the Virgin Mary that she is to be the mother of the Saviour. In this play and the one following, which deals with Joseph's doubts of his wife, every effort is made to emphasize to the audience the doctrine of the miraculous conception and the chastity of Mary ; the author deals with a delicate situation in a masterly manner, and does not degenerate into coarseness. The fourteenth play sets forth the Nativity in considerable detail, and as it was performed by the Tylers'

or Thatchers' Guild, it was perhaps fitting that the stable at
Bethlehem should be represented as a tumble-down
building with a roof much in want of repair.   Joseph
bemoans the poorness of the shelter he is able to procure
for himself and his wife :—

> " All weldand (1) God in Trinite,
> I praye ye, lord, for thy grete myght,
> Unto thy symple servand see,
> Here in this place wher we are pight, (2) oure self allone ;
> Lord, graunte us gode herberow (3) this nyght within this wone. (4)
> For we have sought both uppe and downe
> Thurgh diverse stretis in this cite
> So mekill (5) pepull is comen to towne,
> That we can nowhere herbered be, there is slike prees ; (6)
> For suthe I can no socoure see,
>   but helde (7) us with there bestes.
> And if we here all nyght abide,
> We shall be stormed in this steede ; (8)
> The walles are dune on ilke a side,
> The ruffe is rayned aboven oure hede,
>   Als have I roo." (9)

Joseph goes to procure lights and fuel, and in his absence
the Child is born.

> MARY.—" Now in my sawle grete joie have I,
> I am all cladde in comforte clere,
> Now will be borne of my body
> Both God and man togedir in feere. (10)
>   Blist mott he be !
> Jesu ! my son that is so dere,
>   now borne is he !"

She worships the Child :—

> " Hayle my lord God ! hayle prince of pees !
> Hayle my fadir, and hayle my sone !

(1) Almighty.   (2) Placed.   (3) Lodging.   (4) Abode.   (5) Many.   (6) Such a crowd.
     (7) Shelter.   (8) Place.   (9) Rest.   (10) Company.

Hayle sovereyne sege (1) all sinnes to sesse ! (2)
Hayle God and man in erth to wonne ! (3)
        Hayle ! thurgh whose myght
All this worlde was first begonne, merkness (4) and light."

In the following play we see the shepherds watching their flocks by night. Angels proclaim to them the birth of Christ, and they go to adore him and to make their humble offerings—a brooch with a little tin bell attached, a horn spoon, and some nuts threaded on a ribbon. In successive plays we are shown the various incidents of the life of Christ as narrated in the Gospels, no less than ten pageants being devoted to the representation of the Passion and the Crucifixion. In one of them there is a very curious circumstance ; Satan is introduced as anxious to save the life of Jesus, because, so he argues, if Jesus is killed the Devil's occupation will be gone, as men will be saved by the death of Christ.

The thirty-seventh play is the Harrowing of Hell, one always popular with a mediæval audience, the subject being taken from the apocryphal gospel of Nicodemus. The scene is placed in hell or purgatory, and no doubt a plentiful supply of red fire and a full company of attendant devils added to the realism of the representation. Christ comes to deliver his saints, but leaves the evil-doers in torment. The remaining plays are the Resurrection ; the appearances of Christ to Mary Magdalene, on the road to Emmaus, and to Thomas ; the Purification of the Virgin Mary (which is evidently out of its proper place); the Ascension; the Coming of the Holy Ghost ; the Death of the Virgin ; the departure of the Apostles to preach the Gospel ; the Assumption ; and finally the Day of Judgment.

These plays were performed by the members of the trade

(1) Warrior. (2) Cease. (3) Dwell. (4) Darkness.

guilds of York on the day of the Feast of Corpus Christi, and we fortunately possess a full list (compiled by Roger Burton, the then town clerk of York) of the plays given in the year 1415, and of the guilds that performed them. But besides those already mentioned there were other plays at York of which we have some notices, although the texts appear to be lost. On Midsummer day the play of St. George was performed. There was also a very early play "setting forth the goodness of the Lord's Prayer, in which play all manner of vices and sins were held up to scorn, and the virtues were held up to praise." A guild, composed both of men and women, was formed for the purpose of duly performing this play, and records exist showing that in 1399 the guild had over a hundred members, and an income of £26 5s. 11½d., a large sum in those days. It was to this play that Wicliff, who died in 1384 referred when he wrote of "ye paternoster in Englisch tunge as men segn in ye play of York." It was played up to the year 1572.

Every ten years the guild of Corpus Christi at York gave a performance of the Creed play. The guild seems to have been founded in 1408 for the proper regulation and observance of the Corpus Christi procession, and in 1446 it became possessed, under the will of a chantry priest of York, named William Revetor, who had been warden of the guild, of the Creed play with the books and banners appertaining thereto. The play was given at Lammastide; the last performance took place in 1545, and the guild was dissolved in 1547. An attempt was unsuccessfully made in 1568 to revive the play. The opinion of the ecclesiastical authorities was against it, and they vetoed the performance. The Dean of York, Matthew Hutton, gave as his reason for advising that it should not be played that "though it was plausible to years ago, and would now also of the ignorant sort be well liked, yet now in this happy time of the gospel I know the learned will mislike it." The play had had its day, and was perhaps at the summit of its popularity on the 7th of September in the year 1483, a Sunday, when it was performed before King Richard III., who was then in York for his second Coronation.

The traders' plays were the glory of York, and yearly, at the Feast of Corpus Christi, when days were long and nights were short, the favoured citizens proudly wheeled out their gaudy pageants, and in simple show set forth the Bible story. Though each craft was solely responsible for its own part of the representation, the control of the entire performance was in the hands of the municipality, and a most careful super-vision was exercised over the performances. The authorities not only made provision for the time and places of playing, but did their best to ensure that the plays should go on without interruption or disturbance. On the eve of the plays the mayor issued his proclamation, a copy of which has been preserved, as follows :—

> " Oyez—We command of ye King's behalf and ye Mayor and ye Sheriffs of this City, that no man go armed in this city with swords nor Carlisle axes, nor none other defences in disturbance of ye King's peace and ye play, or hindering of ye procession of Corpore Christi, and that they leave their harness in their Inns, saving knights and squires of worship that have swords borne after them, of pain of forfeiture of their weapon and imprison-ment of their bodies. And that men that bring forth pageants that they play at the places that is assigned therefor and nowhere else, of ye pain of forfeiture to be raised that is ordained there-fore, that is to say 40/. And that men of crafts and all other men that find torches that they come forth in array and in ye manner as it has been used and customed before this time, not

having weapon, carrying tapers of ye pageants. And officers that are keepers of the peace of pain of forfeiture of their franchise and their bodies to prison. And all manner of craftmen that bringeth forth their pageants in order and course by good players well arrayed and openly speaking upon payn losing 100/ to be paid to the chamber without any pardon. And that every player that shall play be ready in his pageant at convenient time, that is to say at the midhour between 4 and 5 of the clock in the morning, and then all other pageants fast following ilk one after other as their course is without tarrying."

In 1399, and again in 1417, it was prescribed that

" For the convenience of the citizens and of all strangers coming to the said feast that all the pageants of the play called Corpus Christi Play should begin to play, first
At the gates of the priory of the Holy Trinity in Mikelgate, next
At the door of Robt. Harpham, next
At the door of the late John Gyseburn, next
At Skeldergate end and North Street end, next
At the end of Conyng Street towards Castelgate, next
At the end of Jubirgate, next
At the door of Henry Wymem deceased in Conyng St., then
At the Common Hall at the end of Conyng Street, then
At the door of Adam del Briggs deceased in Stayne Gate, then
At the end of Stayn Gate at the Minster gates, then
At the end of Girdlergate in Petergate, and lastly
Upon the pavement."

But in 1417 the restriction against playing elsewhere than at the appointed places was removed, and it was ordered that "those persons should be allowed to have the play before their houses who would pay the highest price for the privilege, but that no favour should be shown." This arrangement proved popular, and probably existed as long as the plays did ; in 1519 we find that ambitious citizens, desirous either of entertaining their friends or of attracting notice to their shops, were willing to pay sums varying from

one shilling to four shillings and fourpence for the privilege
of having a play performed at their threshold.

Until the year 1426 the great ecclesiastical function known
as the Corpus Christi procession and the popular miracle
plays had been given on one and the same day, but in that
year, owing to the persuasion of a wandering friar, the City
Council ordered that from thenceforth the plays should be
given on the vigil of the feast of Corpus Christi, and that
the procession should be solemnly made on the day of the
festival.   This, however, did not suit the good citizens
of York, they were not going to have their beloved
plays ousted from the first place, procession or no
procession ; they insisted on having the pageants out on the
old established day, and as usual the popular will prevailed ;
the plays continued to be acted on the day of the festival,
and the procession was postponed to the morrow.

The York plays were essentially the plays of the people,
they were performed by the shopkeepers and artizans of the
city, and, with a single exception, * so far as we know
neither the clergy nor the religious houses had part or lot in
their production.   The cycle is the most complete of any
collection of English miracle plays, and is, further, the only
series that we definitely know was played by the old crafts
and trade guilds at the feast of Corpus Christi.

* The exception is that in the year 1415 the play of the Purification, usually
acted by the hatmakers, the masons, and the labourers, was brought out by the
brothers of the Hospital of St. Leonard.

CHAPTER IV.

The Wakefield Plays.

THE series of miracle plays which we now have to
consider are more closely allied to the plays performed at York than to any of the other extant plays. They
bear distinct traces of a Yorkshire origin, five of them indeed
are almost identical with plays in the York cycle, and it is
probable that at least some of them were acted by the trade
guilds of Wakefield. The cycle is variously known as the
Towneley, Widkirk, Woodkirk, or Wakefield Plays. The
first mentioned title is derived from the fact that the MS.
volume containing the text was long in the library at
Towneley Hall in Lancashire, though how it got there is
not known. The second and third titles are due to a
tradition that the book formerly belonged to the Abbey of
Widkirk, near Wakefield. As a matter of fact no such
abbey is known to have existed, but there was at Woodkirk,
some four miles north of Wakefield, a cell of Augustinian
Canons dependant on the great house of S. Oswald at
Nostel, and it is possible that the compiler of the present
text took some of the plays from a series, now lost, that was
at some time performed at Wakefield and in the surrounding
villages, and borrowed others from various other places,
especially from York. Certain topographical allusions

connect one of the plays, the *Secunda Pastorum,* with the neighbourhood of Wakefield, and two or three plays are earmarked as having been played by certain of the Wakefield trade guilds.   So early as the reign of Henry I. two fairs were held annually at Woodkirk, which would attract large crowds from the surrounding country, and it is more than possible that the plays we are now considering formed one of the attractions.   The men of Wakefield had some reputation as actors, for we find that in the year 1446 players from Wakefield were assisting at the performances in York, and received 6d. for their pains.

The composition of the Wakefield plays has been attributed to the early years of the fifteenth century, but it is possible that some of them have a somewhat more remote origin, while one at least, the Hanging of Judas, is not earlier that the sixteenth century.   The diversity of style and language, indeed, compel the conclusion that the MS. volume is not an acting edition of a settled series of plays, but rather a compilation of various plays that were then in favour in the neighbourhood of Wakefield.

The dialect is certainly, in some of the plays, akin to that of the West Riding rural population, while the incidents introduced into the narrative are such as would appeal to a country audience.   Thus Cain and his servant, in the play of Cain and Abel, are rough country clowns, their language is of the most vulgar description, and the first entrance of Cain, urging on the tired horses and oxen that are drawing his plough, must have caused huge delight to the bucolic spectators.   Indeed, there is but little reverence or feeling in the plays, their feature is the great freedom from restraint, and the boisterousness of the humour.   Even in the play

just mentioned the crime of murder is lightly treated, and
Cain, after being cursed by the offended Deity, turns with
undiminished vigour to indulge in a comic scene with his
servant. The *Secunda Pastorum*, or Second Shepherd's play,
which forms one of the series, is nearly pure fooling, and it
has, with some justice, been described as the first farce in
the English language. It is prefaced by an altogether non-
religious and comic interlude—forming a complete scene or
drama in itself, and having nothing whatever to do with the
subject of the Nativity.

The shepherds are assembled in the fields on Christmas
Eve, and begin in turn to talk of their troubles—they
grumble at the severity of the weather :—

> " Lord, what these weders ar cold, and I am
>   Ylle happyd ; (1)
> I am nere-hande dold, (2) so long have
>   I nappyd ;
> My legys they fold, my fyngers ar chappyd,
> It is not as I wold, for I am al lappyd
>   In sorow."

They complain of the heavy taxes they have to pay, of their
termigant wives, of the disadvantages of matrimony (for all
the world like a modern problem play), of their hard work
and low wages. Presently they lie down to sleep—one
Mak by name with them. As soon as the shepherds are all
soundly sleeping, and loudly snoring, Mak rises very quietly
and slips away with a fat sheep on his back. He hurries
home with his booty and arouses his wife. They discuss
what they shall do with the sheep, and the wife proposes
that they put it in the cradle, and that she shall pretend she
has just been confined :—

(1) Wrapped up.   (2) Stupid.

WIFE.—"A good bowrde (1) have I spied, since thou can none,
  Here shall we hym hyde, to thay (the shepherds) be gone ;
  In my credylle abyde.   Lett me alone,
  And I shalle lyg (2) besyde in chylbed and grone."
Mak agrees.—
    " Thou red ; (3)
    And I shalle say thou was lyght (4)
    Of a knave childe this nyght."

We can imagine the fun caused by their efforts to wrap
up the struggling sheep in baby clothes, and to get it safely
tucked into the cradle, and covered up with the blanket.
At last they succeed, and Mak then returns to the still
sleeping shepherds, and quietly lies down again and pretends
to be fast asleep.   One by one the shepherds wake, and
begin to tell their dreams—how they had dreamt that they
had seen Mak, dressed in a wolf's skin, in the act of carrying
off a sheep.   They wake up the sham sleeper, and Mak says
that he too has had a dream—he has dreamt that his wife
has presented him with a son and heir, and he must needs
go home to see if all be well.   As soon as Mak has gone
the shepherds miss one of the flock, and at once suspecting
Mak, they follow him home and demand admission to his
house.   He bids them

    " Speke soft
   Over a seke woman's heede."

They charge him with having stolen their sheep, but he
indignantly denies the accusation.

  " Now if ye have suspowse (5) to Gille or to me,
   Come and rype (6) oure howse, and then may ye se
    Who had hir.
   If I any shepe fott, (7)
   Aythor cow or stott. (8)
   And Gylle, my wyfe, rose nott

(1) Jest.   (2) Lie.   (3) Advise.   (4) Delivered.   (5) Suspicion.   (6) Ransack.
(7) Fetched.   (8) Young bull.

> Here syn she lade hir.
> As I am true and lele, to God here I pray,
> That this be the fyrst mele that I shalle ete this day."

The shepherds search the house, Mak and his wife using all their wits to keep them from going too near the cradle. Finding no trace of their sheep, they are about to leave the room in despair, but just as they are going out a thought strikes one of them, he turns back and asks leave to kiss the new baby in the cradle.

> " Gyf me lefe him to kys, and lyft up the clout."

Spite of Mak's attempts to prevent him going near the cradle he persists in doing so, lifts up the coverlet, and of course discovers the lost sheep. As a punishment Mak is tossed in a blanket till the shepherds are tired, and as they again lie down to sleep the angel sings " Gloria in Excelsis," and announces the birth of Christ.

> " Ryse hyrdmen heynd, (1) for now is he borne,
> That shall take fro the feynd that Adam had lorne : (2)
> That warloo (3) to sheynd, (4) this night is he borne,
> God is made your freynd : now at this morne
> He behestys,
> At Bedlam go se,
> Ther lygys that fre (5)
> In a cryb full poorely,
> Betwyx two bestys."

The play then proceeds much as in the other shepherds plays that have been preserved. The shepherds try to imitate the angel's song, and then proceed to the stable, where they worship the child Jesus, and make their simple offerings—a bob of cherries, a bird, and a little ball.

The Wakefield cycle consists of thirty-two plays, and commences in the usual way with the Creation, which was

(1) Gentle. (2) Lost. (3) Wizard. (4) Shame. (5) Freeman.

played by the Barbers of the town.　God proclaims himself, and then at once begins to make the world—

> " At the begynnyng of oure dede
>   Make we hevene and erthe, on brede, (1)
>   And lyghtes fayre to se ;
>   For it is good to be so,
>   Darknes from light we parte on two,
>   In tyme to serve and be.
>   Darknes we calle the nyght
>   And lith (2) also the bright,
>   It shalle be as I say ;
>   After my will this is furth broght,
>   Even an morne both ar they wroght,
>   And thus is maid a day."

The second play, which was acted by the Glovers, deals with the episode of Cain and Abel, and in this play we get our first glimpse of the stage clown, a character destined to develop into the fool of Shakespeare and the low comedian of to-day.　It is Garcio, Cain's servant, who claims this distinction.　As he enters he addresses the audience—

> " Alle haylle, alle hayle, bothe blithe and glad
>   For here come I, a mery lad,
>   Be peasse your dyn, (3) my master bad,
>   Or els the deville you spede.
>
> Felowes, here I you forbede
>   To make nother nose ne cry ;
>   Who so is so hardy to do that dede
>   The deville hang hym up to dry.
>   Gedlynges, I am a fulle gret wat, (4)
>
> For if my master com, welcom hym then,
>   Fare welle, for I am gone."

The next play has the Flood for its subject, and consists largely of nagging matches between Noah and his wife.

(1) Abroad.　(2) Light.　(3) Cease your noise.　(4) Man.

She refuses to enter the ark till Noah, after giving her a severe thrashing, pushes her in and bids her take the tiller while he casts the lead. Then follow plays dealing with Abraham and Isaac, Jacob and Esau, the Old Testament prophecies of Christ, Pharoah, the taxing of the world by Cæsar Augustus, the Annunciation, Salutation, and Nativity, the visit of the Wise Men, the flight into Egypt, the slaughter of the Innocents, the Purification, Jesus among the Doctors, John the Baptist, the Last Supper, three plays on the Passion and Crucifixion, the last being coarse and cruel, the Harrowing of Hell, the Resurrection, the appearance of Christ to the disciples, the Ascension, Doomsday, the raising of Lazarus, and the hanging of Judas.

CHAPTER V.

The Chester Plays.

THE Chester plays are more serious in tone than those we have already considered; the humour, though present, is not so boisterous as in the Towneley series, and a didactic tendency is shown in the introduction of an Expositor, who at the end of each play explains its significance and lesson. This is the only series that shows any real effort to serve the religious object to which Miracle Plays were supposed to be directed. The plays are twenty-five in number, and they were acted by the twenty-five trade companies of the city on the Monday, Tuesday, and Wednesday in Whitsun week, from 1268 to 1577, and again in 1600. In the year 1328 the plays received a great impetus by the act of Pope Clement, who decreed a 1000 days of pardon, to which the Bishop of Chester added another month, to everyone who should resort "in peaceable manner with good devotion to hear and see the said plays from time to time as oft as they shall be played within the city." The series commences with the Fall of Lucifer, performed by the Tanners; next the Creation and Fall, by the Drapers; the effect of the representation of the Creation was heightened by sending among the crowd as many strange animals as could be brought together, the creation of birds being imitated by sending up a flight of pigeons. The Deluge was done by the Water-Carriers of the Dee, and was one of the humorous plays, being almost entirely taken up by an altercation between Noah and his wife. The play begins with God's announcement to the patriarch of the coming deluge, and the command to him to build the Ark. Noah replies—

> " O Lorde, I thanke thee, lowde and still,
> That to me arte in suche will,
> And spares me and my howse to spill,
> As I nowe southly (1) fynde.
> Thy byddinge, Lorde, I shall fulfill,
> And never more thee greve nor grill, (2)
> That such grace hath sent me till,
> Amonght all mankinde.

[Turning to his sons and their wives]

> Have done, you men and wemen all,
> Hye you, leste this watter fall,
> To worche this shippe, chamber and hall,
> As God hath bedden us doe."

After this the wife and sons of Noah say a few words relating to their respective duties during the construction. Noah commences the building of the " shippe," and the play proceeds as follows :—

NOAH.

> " Now in the name of God I will begyne
> To make the shippe that we shall in,
> That we maye be ready for to swyme
> At the cominge of the fludde :
> Thes bordes heare I pynne togeither,
> To beare us saffe from the weither,
> That we maye rowe both heither and theither,
> And saffe be from the fludde.
> Of this treey will I make the maste ;
> Tied with cabbelles that will laste,
> With a saile yarde for iche blaste,

(1) Truly. (2) Provoke.

And iche thinge in their kinde :
With toppe-castill, and boe-spritte,
With cords and roppes, I hold all mete
To sayle fourth at the nexte weete ;
This shippe is att an ende.
Wyffe, in this vessel we shall be kepte :
My children and thou, I woulde in ye lepte.

NOAH'S WIFE.

In fayth, Noye, I hade as liffe thou slepte !
For all thy frynish (1) fare,
I will not doe after thy rede. (2)

NOAH.

Good wyffe, doe nowe as I thee bydde.

NOAH'S WIFE.

Be Christe ! not or I see more neede
Though thou stande all the daye and stare."

Noah laments the "crabbed" nature of womankind. The
ark, however, is at length finished, and after enumerating
the animals that are to take refuge therein, Noah
enters the ark with all his family, excepting his wife.
Here considerable liberty is taken with the Biblical
version, and a strange scene is witnessed. Noah's
wife, a person of exceedingly whimsical temper, in
reply to her husband's appeal to her to enter the ark, gives
vent to a volley of strong language, saying that unless her
"gossips" are allowed to go in with her she "will not oute
of this towne," and she tells him to row where he lists, and
to get a new wife. At last the dutiful Japhet compels his
mother to enter by main force, and immediately upon her
entrance she vigorously boxes Noah's ears. He remarks—

"Ha, ha, marye, this is hotte !
It is good for to be still.

(1) Nice.   (2) Advice.

> Ha, children, methinkes my botte remeves,
> Our tarryinge heare hyghlye me greves,
> Over the lande the wather spreades ;
> God doe as he will.
> Ah, greate God, that arte so good,
> That worckes not thy will is wood,
> Nowe all this worlde is one a fludde,
> As I see well in sighte.
> This wyndowe I will shutte anon,
> And into my chamber I will gone,
> Tell this watter, so greate one,
> Be slacked through Thy mighte."

The window of the ark is now closed for a short time, supposed to be during the period of the flood, after which it is opened, and Noah thanks God for granting him such grace. The Almighty replies, and blesses the patriarch, and the play finishes with the following speech by God :—

> " My bowe betweyne you and me
> In the firmament shal be,
> By verey tocken that you shall see,
> That suche vengance shall cease.
> That man ne woman shall never more
> Be wasted with watter, as hath before ;
> But for synne that greveth me sore.
> Therfore this vengance was.
>
> .   .   .   .   .   .
>
> My blessinge Noye, I give thee heare,
> To thee, Noye, my servante deare ;
> For vengance shall noe more appeare,
> And nowe farewell, my darlinge deare."

The examples already given of the literature of the miracle plays have been of a humorous nature. I now want to draw attention to these old playwrights' power of building up a tragic and pathetic play, and for this purpose I take the play of the " Sacrifice of Isaac," the fourth play in the

Chester series :—God calls to Abraham, and bids him offer his son as a sacrifice.   Abraham replies—

> "My Lorde, to thee is myne intente
> Ever to be obediente ;
> That sonne that thou to me hast sente,
>   Offer I will to thee ;
> And fulfill thy commanndemente,
> With heartie will, as I am kente, (1)
> Highe God, Lorde omnipotènte,
>   Thy byddinge done shal be.
> My meanye (2) and my children eich (3) one
> Lenges (4) at home, both alle and one
> Save Isaake, my sonne, with me shall gone
>   To a hill heare besyde."

Abraham then says to Isaac :—

> " Make thee readye, my deare darlinge,
> For we must doe a littill thinge.
> This woode upon thy backe it bringe,
>   We maye no longer abyde.
> A sworde and fier that I will take ;
> For sacrefice me behoves to make ;
> Gode's byddinge will I not forsake,
>   But ever obediente be.

ISAAC.—Father, I am all readye
>   To doe your byddinge moste mekelye,
>   To beare this woode full beane (5) am I,
>   As you commaunded me.

ABRAHAM.—O Isaake, my darlinge deare,
>   My blessinge nowe I give thee heare,
>   Take up this faggote with good cheare,
>   And on thy backe it bring ;
>   And fier with us I will take.

ISAAC.—Your byddinge I will not forsake ;
>   Father, I will never slake
>   To fulfill your byddinge."

(1) Taught.   (2) Company.   (3) Each.   (4) Remain.   (5) Obedient.

They go to the place of sacrifice, where Isaac, being frightened, says :—

> " Father, I am full sore affeared
> To see you beare that drawne sworde :
> I hope for all myddel earde (1)
> You will not slaye your childe."

ABRAHAM.—Dreede thee not, my childe, I reade ;
Our Lorde will sende of his godheade
Some manner of beaste unto this steade,
Either tame or wild."

Soon after, Abraham tells Isaac that he must kill him.

ISAAC.—" Alas ! father, is that your will,
Your owine child for to spill
Upon this hille's brinke ?
If I have treasspasede in anye degree,
With a yarde you may beat me ;
Put up your sorde, if your will be,
For I am but a childe.

ABRAHAM.—O, my deare sonne, I am sorye
To doe to thee this great anoye :
Gode's commaundmente doe must I,
His workes are ever full mylde.

ISAAC.—Woulde God my mother were here with me !
Shee woulde kneele downe upon her knee,
Prainge you, father, if it may be,
, For to save my life."

Abraham replies that he must obey the divine command, and Isaac then asks his father's blessing.

> " Father, seinge you muste nedes doe soe,
> Let it passe lightlie, and over goe ;
> Kneelinge on my kneeyes towe,
> You blessinge on me spreade.

ABRAHAM.—My blessinge, deere son, give I thee
And thy mother's with hart free
The blessing of the Trinitie
My deare sone, on thee lighte.

(1) The world.

ISAAC.—Father, I praye you, hyde my eyne
That I see not the sorde so keyne,
Your strocke, father, woulde I not seene,
Leste I againste it grylle." (1)

Isaac is then bound and laid on the altar.

ISAAC.—" A ! mercye, father, why tarye you soe?
Smyte of my head, and let me goe ;
I pray you rydd me of my woe,
For nowe I take my leve.

ABRAHAM.—Ah, sonne ! my harte will breake in three,
To heare thee speake such words to me.
Jesu ! on me thou have pittye,
That I have moste in mynde.

ISAAC.—Nowe, father, I see that I shall dye :
Almightie God in magestie !
My soule I offer unto thee ;
Lorde, to it be kinde."

Abraham takes the sword, and is about to cut off his son's head, when an angel appears and stays his hand. He points out a lamb entangled in some briars, which Abraham offers in sacrifice. God appears and utters his blessing upon Abraham and his seed, and the play is concluded by the Expositor explaining the moral.

" This deed you see done here in this place,
In example of Jesu done it was,
That for to win mankind to grace
Was sacrificed on the roode.
By Abraham, I maie understande
The father of heaven that can fand, (2)
With his sonne's bloode to breake that bande, (3)
That the devill had broughte us to.
By Isaake understande I maie,
Jesu, that was obediente aye,
His father's will to work alwaie,
And death for to confounde."

At this point a messenger riding through the crowd of

(1) Rebel.   (2) Find.   (3) Curse.

spectators arrives at the pageant to announce the coming of
the next play in the series, and the Barbers and Wax Chandlers
who acted the Sacrifice of Isaac, go off in their pageant to
re-enact the play in another part of the city. The next play,
which is on the subject of Balaam and his Ass, and is not to
be found in any other English collection, concludes the
representation of the Old Testament history, and in the next
pageant the Salutation and the Nativity are played. Then
comes the Shepherds' play, which, as in other cycles, is an
elaborate picture of country life. In succeeding plays the
main incidents of the life of Christ are set out; then we
come again, in the nineteenth of the series, to the ever popular
Harrowing of Hell, which, like the play of the Judgment
Day, was made the medium of much topical allusion. Thus,
we find that one of the dwellers in the infernal regions is a
woman who tells the audience that—

> " Some tyme I was a tavernere,
> A gentill gossipe and a taptere,
> Of wyne and ale a trustie brewer,
>   Which wo hath me wroughte ;
> Of cannes I kepte no trewe measuer,
> My cuppes I soulde at my pleasuer.
> Deceaving manye a creature,
>   Tho my ale were naughte."

She had adulterated her ale, and brewed thin beer, offences
of too grave a nature to permit any pardon, and in con-
sequence she is left to the tender mercies of the devil, who
exclaims—

> " Welckome dere ladye, I shall thee wedd,
> For many a heavye and droncken head,
> Cause of thy ale were broughte to bed
>   Farre worse than anye beaste."

The following proclamation contains the earliest authentic

mention we have of the Chester plays, and gives an interesting account of the origin of the plays and the manner of their performance :—

> " The proclamation for Whitsone plays, made by Wm. Newall, clarke of the Pendice, 24 Hen. 8., Wm. Snead, 2nd yere maior.
>
> For as much as of old time, not only for the augmentation and increase of the holy and catholick faith of our Saviour Jesus Christ, and to exort the mindes of comon people to good devotion and holsome doctrine thereof, but also for the comenwelth and prosperity of this city, a play and declaration of divers storyes of the Bible, beginning with the creation and fall of Lucifer, and ending with the generall Judgment of the World, to be declared and played in the Whitsonne weeke, was devised and made by one Sʳ Henry Frances, sometyme monck of this monastrey disolved, who obtayning and got of Clement, then bishop of Rome, a thousand dayes of pardon, and of the bishop of Chester at that time forty days of pardon, graunted from thensforth to every person resorting in peaceble manner with good devotion to heare and see the sayd plays from tyme to tyme, as oft as they shall be played within the sayd citty (and that every person or persons disturbing the sayd playes in any manner wise to be accused by the authority of the said pope Clement's bulls untill such tyme as he or they be absolved thereof), which playes were devised to the honor of God by John Arnway, then Maior of this citty of Chester, his brethren and whole community thereof, to be brought forth, declared, and played at the cost and charges of the craftsmen and occupations of the said citty, which hitherunto have from tyme to tyme used and performed the same accordingly.
>
> Wherfore Mr. Maior, in the King's name, stratly chargeth and comandeth that every person or persons, of what estate, degree, or condition so ever he or they be, resorting to the said playes, do use themselves peacibli, without making any assault, affray, or other disturbance whereby the same plays shall be disturbed, and that no manner of person or persons, whosoever he or they be, do use or weare any unlawfull weapons within the precinct of the sayd citty during the time of the sayd playes (not only upon payn of cursing by authority of the sayd pope Clement's bulls) but also upon payne of enprisonment of their bodyes and making fine to the King at Mr. Maior's pleasure."

CHAPTER VI.

The Coventry Plays.

COVENTRY shared with York the distinction of being the supreme home of the English miracle play. A complete cycle of plays has been preserved which are said, on somewhat inconclusive authority, to have been acted at Coventry at the Feast of Corpus Christi. These plays are included in the Cottonian Collection in the British Museum, and are ascribed to Coventry on the strength of an inscription by Sir Robert Cotton's librarian. If they did really belong to Coventry, the plays are those that were acted by the religious community of the Grey Friars, and are not in any way connected with the plays or pageants which we know were exhibited by the trading companies of the town. The conclusion of the prologue to the plays indicates rather a series of plays for performance at Corpus Christi generally than at any particular place :—

> " A Sunday next if that we may
> At VI. of the bell we gynne our play
> In N——town, wherfor we pray
> That God now be your spede. Amen."

The M.S. probably dates from the time of Henry VI., or about the year 1468, and consists of forty-two plays, which were not, however, all acted in any one year. The practice was to perform the first twenty-eight plays, covering the period from the Creation of the World to the Betrayal of Christ, one year, and the remaining plays, up to Doomsday, the next year. The plays, as might be expected if they were acted by ecclesiastics, have a higher and more religious tone than those of the other series ; the humour is less exuberant, and altogether the plays seem to have been performed with some idea of illustrating to the people the great truths of the Christian religion. Eight of the plays are founded on the spurious gospels in the New Testament Apochrypha.

Coventry does not, however, depend for its histrionic fame on the plays included in the Cottonian M.S. Quite apart from these the town was peculiarly famous for its religious dramas.

From a very early date the various trading companies of Coventry acted miracle plays, and continued to do so until the year 1580, when the performances were temporarily suppressed. In 1584 an attempt was made to revive them, and a new play on the Destruction of Jerusalem was provided to add fresh interest to the representation. Very considerable expense was incurred on account of this revival, no less than £13 6s. 8d. being paid to the author of the new play, but it was all in vain. The days of the miracle play were numbered ; the popular mind was beginning to require more than the simple fare they provided; and the year 1591 witnessed the last performance of miracle plays at Coventry. Dugdale, in his "Antiquities of Warwickshire," which was published about 1656, states that he had himself spoken with old people who had in their younger days witnessed the miracle plays at Coventry at the festival of Corpus Christi, and who told him that great crowds of people were wont to assemble from far and near to see the performances. Hey-

wood, in his play, "The Four P's," written in 1530, refers
to the Coventry plays—

"For as good hap would have it chance,
This devil and I were of olde acquaintance ;
For oft, in the play of Corpus Christi,
He hath play'd the devil at Coventrie."

The texts of the plays represented by the various trade
guilds have been lost, with the exception of that belonging
to the Shearmen and Taylors, which is on the subject of the
birth of Christ, with which it deals in a more extensive
manner than was usual in miracle plays. This play not only
sets forth the Nativity, but includes the visit of the Wise Men
from the East, the flight of the Holy Family into Egypt, and
the Massacre of the Innocents. At the commencement of
the play the prophet Isaiah foretells the coming of the
Messiah, and then the angel Gabriel announces to the Virgin
Mary the approaching birth of her son Jesus. The shepherds
are introduced, and when the child is born they adore him
and, as usual, offer their gifts, in this instance—a pipe, a hat,
and a pair of mittens. Then Herod enters, and is told by a
messenger, who speaks in most villainous French, of the
birth of one who is to be the King of the Jews. Herod is,
of course, depicted as a braggart and boaster of the most
exaggerated kind; his pride and his furious ravings being
perhaps more pronounced in this play than in any other
miracle play in which the character was introduced. As this
play was perhaps acted so late as the year 1591, and
Shakespeare was probably living at Stratford, only a few
miles from Coventry, till within a few years of that time, it
has been thought not improbable that he witnessed some
late performance of the play, and that the references he

makes in his own dramas were suggested by his recollections of the violent rhetoric and action of the Coventry Herod.* For this reason, if for no other, we may justify some little consideration of Herod as represented by the Coventry tailors. He was dressed to represent a Saracen in a gown of gaudy colours, and bore in his hands, which were covered with red gloves or gauntlets, a sceptre and a painted wooden sword. His face was concealed behind a highly-coloured mask, and on his head he wore an iron helmet with an ornamental crest. The accounts of the Coventry companies contain many curious items in connection with this character :—

> " Item, to a peyntour for peyntyng the fanchon and Herode's face—x*d*.
> Item, peyd to a peynter for peyntyng and mendyng of Herode's heed—iiij*d*.
> Item, paid for a gowen to Arrode—vij*s*. iij.
> Item, paid for peynttyng and stenyng theroff—vj*s*. iiij*d*.
> Item, paid for iij platis to Heroddi's crest of iron—vj*d*.
> Item, paid for colour and coloryng of Arade—iiij."

Altogether there is no reason to doubt that Herod when he leapt upon the stage presented a sufficiently gorgeous and terrible appearance, and certainly his words do not belie his looks. He announces himself as "the myghtyst conquerowre that ever walkid on grownd," and, as some justification for the statement, says—

> " Magog and Madroke bothe thes did I confownde,
> And in this bryght bronde there bonis I brak on sunder,
> That all the wyde worlde on those rappis did wonder."

He tells his audience that it is he who is the cause of

---

* Compare *Hamlet*, Act iii, scene 2 ; *Antony and Cleopatra*, Act iii, scene 3 ; *Merry Wives of Windsor*, Act ii, scene 1.

lightning and thunder, and of earthquakes ; that he is prince of "purgatorre," and chief captain of hell. His rage when he is angered is something to be remembered, for not content with stamping and raving in the circumscribed limits of the stage, he on occasion descends from the platform and rages among the crowd of onlookers. When he is informed that the wise men from the East have escaped from his messengers his fury is boundless :—

> "I stampe, I stare, I loke all abowt,
> Myght I them take I schuld them bren at a glede, (1)
> I ren, I rawe, (2) and now I am wode, (3)
> A that these velen trayturs hath mard this my mode,
> They schal be hangid yf I ma cum them to."

And then occurs this curious stage direction : " Here Erode ragis in the pagond, and in the strete also." The massacre of the young children then takes place, in spite of the desperate resistance offered by the mothers of Bethlehem, and the bodies are brought to Herod in a cart. On hearing that Jesus is not among the slain, but has escaped with Joseph and Mary into Egypt, the King again falls into a violent passion, orders his horse to be brought, and ends the play by riding away through the crowd of spectators as if in pursuit of the Holy Family.

As a contrast to the fury and bluster of Herod, let us conclude this short account of the "Shearmen and Taylors' play" by quoting the pretty and tender little lullaby sung by the mothers over their infants just before the massacre :—

> "Lully, lulla, thw littell tiné child ;
> By by, lully, lullay, thw littell tiné child ;
> By by, lulla, lullay.

(1) Burn on live coals. (2) Rave. (3) Mad.

O sisters, too ! how may we do
  For to preserve this day
This pore yongling, for whom we do singe
  By by, lully, lullay.

Herod, the King, in his raging,
  Chargid he hath this day
His men of might, in his owne sight,
  All yonge children to slay.

That wo is me, pore child, for thee,
  And ever morne and say,
For thi parting nether say nor sing
  By by, lully, lullay.

CHAPTER VII.

Other English Miracle Plays.

BESIDES the miracle plays acted at York, Wakefield, Chester, and Coventry, there were others of a similar nature performed in every part of England. Not only in the centres of population were these plays popular; they were represented either regularly or occasionally in a large number of the smaller towns and villages, and it would perhaps not be very wide of the mark to say that there was no part of England in which a miracle play was not acted some time during the fourteenth, fifteenth, and sixteenth centuries.

In London the performances seem to have been mainly in the hands of the parish clerks, and of the scholars or choristers of St. Paul's. In 1378 we find the latter body petitioning Richard II. to prohibit some ignorant and inexpert persons from acting "The History of the Old Testament," to the great prejudice of the petitioners, who had been at considerable expense in preparing for a public representation of the play at the following Christmas. The parish clerks were wont to yearly perform a series of miracle plays in the fields lying to the north of the city, now known as Clerkenwell and Skinner's Well. On July 18th, 19th, and 20th, 1390, they played at Clerkenwell before Richard II. and his Queen, and a great concourse of the nobles and dignitaries of the realm, and in the year 1409 it is recorded that they played at Skinner's Well a drama which lasted for

4

eight days, and extended from the Creation of the World to Doomsday. This performance, Stow tells us, was given in the presence of "the most part of the nobles and gentles in England." Weever, referring to these plays in his "Funeral Monuments," says "They call this Corpus Christi play in my country, which I have seen acted at Preston and Lancaster, and last of all at Kendall, in the beginning of the reign of King James; for which the townsmen were sore troubled; and upon good reasons the play finally supprest, not only there, but in all other towns of the kingdom." Another mention of the Kendal performances, together with a curious testimonial to the value of the miracle plays as teachers of Scripture knowledge, is found in the writings of the Rev. John Shaw, who, in 1644, was in spiritual charge of the parish of Cartmel, in Lancashire. He says :—"One day an old man about sixty, sensible enough in other things, and living in the parish of Cartmel, coming to me about some business, I told him that he belonged to my care and charge, and I desired to be informed in his knowledge of religion ;—I asked him how many Gods there were ; he said he knew not ;—I, informing him, asked him again how he thought to be saved; he answered he could not tell, yet he thought that was a harder question than the other ;—I told him that the way to salvation was by Jesus Christ, God-man, who, as He was man, shed His blood for us on the crosse, &c. ;—Oh, sir, said he, I think I heard of that man you speak of once in a play at Kendall called Corpus Christ play, where there was a man on a tree, and blood ran downe &c. ; and after, he professed that he could not remember that ever he heard of salvation by Jesus Christ but in that play."

THE BEVERLEY MINSTRELS.

(From a Pillar in S. Mary's Church, Beverley.)

At Newcastle-on-Tyne there was a cycle of sixteen plays performed from 1426 to 1589, of which only one, "Noah and the Flood," has been preserved; and, during the fifteenth century, a series of fourteen plays was acted in Dublin, the text of one only, the play of "Abraham and Isaac," being known to-day. Of the grand cycle of thirty-six plays which we know was regularly represented at Beverley the whole of the text has been lost, and the same may be said of the great majority of English miracle plays, for, with the exception of the four series described in former chapters, only about a dozen separate plays are now extant. Three of these are contained in a fifteenth century manuscript preserved in the Bodleian Library, and are specially interesting as the remains of the old Cornish religious plays. They are written in Cymric, and the subjects are :—"The Origin of the World," "The Passion of our Lord," and "The Resurrection." Another Cornish play was that of "Adam and Seth," which was also the subject of one of the Beverley series. These Cornish miracle plays were not acted on moveable pageants or temporary platforms, as was the custom in other parts of England, but in round enclosures of earth or stone, relics perhaps of the Roman amphitheatres, or of the more ancient Grecian theatres. Richard Carew, in his "Survey of Cornwall," dated 1602, gives an interesting description of the performance of miracle plays in these Cornish rounds :— "The Guary miracle, in English a miracle play, is a kinde of Enterlude, compiled in Cornish out of some Scripture history with that grossness which accompanied the Romanes *vetus Comedia.* For representing it they raise an earthen amphi-theatre in some open field, having the diameter of his enclosed playne some forty or fifty feet. The country

people flock from all sides, many miles off, to hear and
see it ; for they have therein devils and devices, to delight
as well the eye as the eare ; the players conne not their
parts without booke, but are prompted by one called the
ordinary, who followeth at their back with the book in his
hand, and telleth them softly what they must pronounce aloud.
Which manner once gave occasion to a pleasant conceyted
gentleman of practising a mery pranke ; for he, undertaking,
perhaps of set purpose, an actor's roome, was accordingly
lessoned beforehand by the Ordinary that he must say after
him.   His turn came.   Quoth the Ordinary, 'Goe forth,
man, and show thyself.'   The gentleman steps out upon the
stage, and like a bad clarke in Scripture matters, cleaving
more to the letter than the sense, pronounced those words
aloud.   'Oh,' says the fellow softly in his eare, 'you marre
all the play.'   And with this his passion, the actor makes
the audience in like sort acquainted.   Herein the prompter
falles to flat rayling and cursing in the bitterest terms he
could devise ; which the gentleman with a set gesture and
countenance still soberly related, untill the Ordinary, driven
at last into a madde rage, was faine to give over all.   Which
trousse, though it broke off the Enterlude, yet defrauded
not the beholders, but dismissed them with a great deale
more sport and laughter than twenty such Guaries could
have afforded."

Miracle plays were also acted at Leeds, where a cycle in
verse was performed by the trade-guilds at the festival of
Corpus Christi, and also at Leicester, Reading, Lincoln,
Worcester, Shrewsbury, Tewkesbury, and a great number of
other places.   In 1487 Henry VII. was entertained at
Winchester with a play called "The Harrowing of Hell, or

the Triumphant Entry of Christ into the Infernal World,"
by the choir boys of Hyde Abbey and St. Swithin's Priory,
two local monasteries. Just a hundred years before the
Bishop of Winchester had forbidden the performance of
plays in the cemetery of his cathedral. At Cambridge,
in 1350, a play on "The Children of Israel" was acted, and
in 1416 the play of St. George of Cappadocia was performed
at Windsor before Henry V. and his guest, the Emperor
Sigismund. In the seaport of Kingston-upon-Hull the play
of "Noah" was performed annually, for over 300 years, on
Plough Monday, the Monday after Twelfth Night, by the
members of the Shipmasters' or Mariners' Guild, which still
exists as the Trinity House. The performance was preceded
by the celebration of Mass in the parish church, which was
dedicated to the Holy Trinity, and where the "Ark" was
kept out of harm's way during the year by being suspended
from the roof of the church. This ark was fashioned on
the model of an ordinary ship, with mast and rigging, and
round the sides of the vessel boards were hung, on which
were painted pictures of the animals and birds that were
supposed to take refuge within. The records of the Guild
for the year 1591 show that in that year a new ark was
purchased at a cost of £7 4s. 11d.

The Miracle Play seems to have been also performed in
Scotland, for we find records of representations in Aberdeen
from 1442 to 1531, and in Edinburgh in 1503 and 1554.

In addition to the fixed and regular performances which
we have hitherto been describing, there were others given
by bands of strolling players who wandered over the country,
either assisting in the local plays or giving performances on
their own account wherever they were allowed to do so.

Thus, players from Coventry are found performing at Bristol in 1570, and actors from London, Donnington, and Wakefield were playing in the York plays in 1446-7, the Londoners receiving the sum of six shillings and eightpence for their pains, while the Donnington and Wakefield men were rewarded with one shilling and sixpence respectively. After the Reformation the Miracle Plays lost their popularity, other forms of drama were ousting them from public favour, and with the close of the sixteenth century they practically ceased to be performed in England.

CHAPTER VIII.

The Production of a Miracle Play.

THE records of the cities that were noted for their miracle plays, especially those of York and Coventry, and the accounts and minute books of the various crafts and trade guilds, contain so many entries relating to the plays, that it is tolerably easy to ascertain the manner in which a miracle play was produced, and how the details of the performances were arranged. The object of the present chapter is to consider the miracle play as it was staged and acted, quite apart from any literary or religious features, or in other words to deal solely with what may be termed the stage-management of the performance. When a company or guild reached a position of sufficient importance and opulence, it aspired to share with the other companies and guilds in the responsibilities and glories of the Easter, Whitsuntide, or Corpus Christi festivals. The first duty of the members was to apply to the city authority for permission to produce a play, and for the allotment to them of a subject. This sanction was not always easily obtained, as the inclusion of a new play in the settled cycle meant a certain amount of disarrangement of the series. Each guild was very jealous of any interference with the subject of its own particular pageant, and resented very keenly any attempt to deprive it of any portion of its play. The new comer could be accommodated in one of three ways—it could either undertake an entirely new play on a subject not dealt with in the pageants of the other companies ; or, a play already belonging to the series, and dealing with several incidents in the Scriptural narrative, could be split up, and one or more incidents be entrusted to the applicants for treatment by them as a separate play ; or, the new guild could arrange for the transfer to it of a play previously performed by a guild that, owing to poverty or other reasons, could not longer properly support its part of the series. This last was, perhaps, the most frequent method of acquiring a right to a play, and there are records in the registers of York and other cities of such transfers having been approved by the authorities.

The responsibilities of the guild were great. Once a play had been allotted to it, it was bound under severe penalties to worthily and regularly sustain the burden. This was no light task, for the cost of producing a play was very considerable, and had to be borne by the members of the guild, with the assistance, in some cases, of contributions from the members of a guild that did not bring out a pageant of its own. Thus, in York, on the 21st November, 1517, it was ordered "that for a peace to be had betwixt the Skinners and the Vestment Makers, that from henceforth the Vestment Makers shall pay yearly to the bringing forth of the Skinner's pageant, every master eight pence, and every journeyman fourpence, and no more, to be paid without denial yearly to the Chamberlain's hands afore the feast of Whitsunday, and then the Skinners to receive it at the Chamberlain's hands, and they not to be charged with the representation of their pageant." At Coventry we find similar enactments ; thus, the Bakers, Chandlers, and Cooks were ordered to contribute towards the expenses of the

Smith's play, which was the Trial and Crucifixion of Christ ; and, in 1548, the Cappers received 3s. 4d. from the Whittawer's Company for the "hyer of our pageand," and for several years the Cardmakers and Sadlers paid 13s 4d. towards the cost of the Capper's pageant. The penalty for failing to produce a pageant was heavy, as will be seen from entries in the Coventry accounts for the years 1428 and 1459. In the former year the Smiths were ordered to "occupie the said pachand (pageant) forthe evry yere upon the payne of xli (ten pounds) to be payed at evry defaute to the use of the chambur," and on the later date it was ordained that "every Craft that hath pagant to play in, that the pagant be made ready and brought forth to play upon pain of 100 shillings, to be raised of four masters of the Craft that so offend."

To meet the expenses incurred by a guild in taking part in the miracle plays, a yearly rate, varying in the different guilds from a penny to fourpence, was levied on every member. In 1479, the Shipmen's or Mariners' Guild at York ordered that every member of the guild "sailing as master with a freeman, pay yearly twopence, and he that sails as a fellow pay a penny, to the sustenation and uphold-ing, as well of the pageant of Noah, as of the bringing forth and burning of certain torches before the shrine of Corpus Christi yearly," In some places, payment of pageant money, as this yearly levy was called, was enforced on all persons exercising any craft or trade, whether members of a guild or not ; the "foreigners," or non-members, having to pay twice as much as the admitted craftsmen, and the collection was continued long after the original object had passed into oblivion. At York, for instance, pageant money survived

till the year 1771, or nearly 200 years after the miracle plays
had ceased to be performed.

For the purpose of collecting the pageant money, and of
generally superintending the performance of its play, each
craft appointed certain of its members, generally two in
number, to act as Pageant Masters. These officials were
elected some little time before the day or days fixed for the
festival, and, besides having to get in the money, they were
entrusted with the spending of it, and had to subsequently
account to their craft for every penny received and paid.

When a play, or a subject for a play, had been duly
assigned to a guild, the next step was to procure the book
of words. Where the play was to be an entirely new one,
some learned man, generally a monk or a priest, was
commissioned to write it. We have seen how at Coventry
a new play was provided in 1584, on the subject of the
Destruction of Jerusalem ; the author was an Oxford scholar
named Smythe, one of the earliest literary members of the
great Smith family, and he founded his play in a great
measure on the chronicles of Josephus. Here is the entry
from the city accounts of the payment made to him for his
play :—"Paid to Mr. Smythe of Oxford, the 15 day of
April, 1584, for his pains for writing of the tragedy,
£13 6s. 8d." Where the play to be produced was an old
one, the text had, perhaps, to be revised, and the parts for
each character had to be written out. Thus we get such
items in the accounts as the following :—

" Paid to Robert Crowe for makyng of the boke for the paggen,
20s."
" John Green for writing of the play booke, 5s."
" Item, for amending Noye Pyleh, iiijd."
" Item, payd to Nicholas Helpby for wrytg the play, vijd."

A most important personage was the prompter, or "bearer of the original," who perhaps also filled the office of stage manager, and instructed the performers in their parts. In 1494, the Smith's Company of Coventry paid this functionary 6d., which seems but a small remuneration for such a responsible post; in 1584, the honorarium had risen to 2s., which was the sum paid to "Robert Lawton for kepynge of the booke."

Very great care was exercised in choosing and training the actors. From the municipal records at York we learn that the Council itself looked after this department, for on the 3rd of April, 1476, it was ordained—"That yearly in the time of Lent there shall be called before the mayor for the time being four of the most cunning, discreet, and able players within this city, to search, hear, and examine all the players and plays and pageantes throughout all the artificers belonging to the Corpus Christi play. And all such as they shall find sufficient in personne and cunning, to the honour of the City, and worship of the said Crafts for to admit and able; and all other insufficient persons either in cunning, voice, or person to discharge, remove, and avoid. And that no player that shall play in the said Corpus Christi play be conduct and retained to play but twice on the day of the said play, and that he or they so playing play not over twice the same day, upon pain of 40s. to forfeit unto the chamber as often times as he or they shall be found in default in the same."

The play and the players having been selected the rehearsals commenced ; the number varied according to the newness and difficulty of the play; for the new play at Coventry in 1584, the Smiths thought six rehearsals necessary, while the Cappers were content with five. For a play that had previously been performed by a guild a couple of rehearsals seem to have been all that were required. These were conducted either in some open space or in the halls of the guilds, or in rooms hired for the purpose.

> " Paid for Sent Marye Hall to reherse there, ijd. "

The actors were paid small sums in respect of their attendances at rehearsals, and as they took place early in the morning, also had breakfast provided for them, as well as a supply of liquid refreshment. Eating and drinking, as we shall see later on, formed an ever present feature of both rehearsals and public performances.

> " Payd to the players for rehearsal—Imprimis, to God, ii.s. viij.d. ; itm. to Pilate his wife, ii.s. ; itm. to the Devil and Judas, i.s. vi.d. "
>
> " Paid to the plears at the fyrst reherse, ij.s. vj.d ; Paid for ale, iiij.d. "

A full account has been preserved of the expenses incurred by the Smiths of Coventry, in 1490, in rehearsing their pageant of the Trial and Passion of Christ. They were as follows :—

> " This is the expens of the furste reherse of our players in Ester weke.
>
> | | | | | |
> |---|---|---|---|---|
> | Imprimis in Brede, | - | - | - | iiij.d. |
> | Itm. in Ale, | - | - | - | viij.d. |
> | Itm. in Kechyn | - | - | - | xiij.d. |
> | Itm. in Vynegre, | - | - | - | jd. |
>
> Item Payd at the Second Reherse in Whyttson weke, in brede, ale, and kechyn, ii.s. iiij.d. "

Each craft had its own moveable stage or pageant, on which it represented the play allotted to it. These pageants were erections or scaffolds upon either four or six wheels, and were divided into two parts or rooms, an upper and a

lower. The upper one, which was either open at the top
and sides, or covered in with a canopy, arches, battlements,
or the like, was the stage ; while the lower room, which was
enclosed with painted cloths, served as a dressing and
retiring room for the performers. Every portion of the
vehicle that was open to public view was highly ornamented
in colours. On some pageants there was a raised platform
at the back of the stage, on which certain parts of the
action took place ; in the floor of the stage were trap
doors communicating with the lower room, through which
the performers ascended and descended. In some cases,
as we shall see, the descent was supposed to be to the
infernal regions, while the ascent from the stage to the
raised platform at the back counterfeited the passage from
earth to Heaven. The floor of the stage was strewn with
rushes.

The pageants were not flimsily constructed erections, nor
intended for merely temporary use. They were solidly
and carefully built of wood and iron, and evidently lasted
for a number of years. Entries showing repairs to pageants
are very numerous, as well as those of payments for their
decoration. The accounts of the Company of Smiths of
Coventry contain the following :—

1462. " Item, expende at the fest of Corpus Christi yn reparacion of
the pagent, that ys to say, a peyre of new whelys, the pryce
viij.s. ; item, for naylys and ij. hokys for the sayd pagiente,
iiij.d."

1470. " Item, ij. clampys of iron for the pagent viij.d., item, ij. legges
to the pagent and the workemanship withall, vjd."

1471. " Expenses for burneysshing and peyntyng of the fanes to the
pagent xx.d. ; expenses to a joyner for workemanshipp to the
pagent, vij.d."

1480. " Item, paid for ij. peyre newe whelis, viij.s. ; expenses at the

settyng on of hem, vij.d. ; item, for byndyng of thame, viij.d. ;
    payd to a carpenter for the pagent rowf, vj.d."
1499. "Item, paid for havyng oute of the paygant and swepying
    thereof and havyng in, and for naylles and ij. claspes of iron,
    and for mendyng of a claspe that was brokon, and for coterellis
    and for a bordor to the pagaunte, xix.d."
1554. "Item, payd to payntter for payntyng of the pagent tope,
    xxij.d."

When the pageants were not in use they were kept in
buildings hired for the purpose, which were known as
pageant-houses. In York these buildings appear to have
been the property of the Corporation, and to have been
hired by the various guilds at a yearly rent of one shilling
each. In 1502 the Council ordered that the Coopers should
have sufficient and convenient room for their pageant within
the pageant-house of the Baxters. The accounts of the
Coventry Company of Smiths contain frequent items relating
to the repairing and rent of their pageant-house :—

"Item, paide to James Bradshawe for mendynge the pageant-
    howse doores, iiij.d. ; item, to Christofer Burne for a key and
    settynge on the locke on the doore, v.d. ; item, paide to
    Baylyffe Emerson for halfe-yeres rent of the pageant-house,
    ij.s. vj.d. ; item, gyven to Bryan, a sharman, for his good wyll
    of the pageante-house, x.d."

In 1586, the Smiths sold their pageant-house for a pound,
and the pageant itself for forty shillings.

As the time for the playing drew near, proclamations
were issued by the authorities ordering all evil disposed
persons to leave the town, announcing the precautions that
would be taken against riots and disturbances during the
performances, and settling the order of the plays and other
details. Specimens of these proclamations have already been
given in the chapters dealing with the York and Chester
plays. On the evening before the plays the various stations

appointed for the performances were marked out by banners bearing the city arms, and probably scaffolds or tiers of seats were erected for the accommodation of those of the better class of spectators who could not obtain places in the windows of the neighbouring houses.

At length the great day dawns. The narrow streets of the ancient city are crowded with holiday folks, who have come from far and near to see the plays. Lords and ladies from the castles and great houses of the county are here, with hosts of knights, esquires, men-at-arms, and grooms. Farmers have jogged into the city with wives or daughters; monks, palmers, pilgrims, jongleurs, mountebanks and pedlers, merchants, tradesmen and apprentices, all jostle and elbow each other in their anxiety to get a good place. The members of the crafts, who have assembled at the appointed spot almost before sunrise, are busy dressing for their parts, and putting the finishing touches to the finery of their pageants; all eagerly awaiting the signal to set out on their triumphant progress through the city. But first gaily accoutred heralds, or *vexillatores*, ride through the streets, and with sound of trumpets read the Banes, or Bans, which are the time honoured prologue to the performances. The Banes read before the Chester plays on the 4th of June, 1600, have been preserved. A few verses will serve to show their nature :—

> " Reverende lordes and ladyes all,
>   That at this tyme here assembled bee,
>   By this messauge understande you shall
>   That some tymes there was mayor of this citie
>   Sir John Arnway, Knighte, who most worthilye
>   Contented himselfe to sett out in playe
>   The devise of one Done Rondall, monke of Chester Abbey.

This moonke, moonke-like, in Scriptures well seene,
In storyes travilled with the beste sorte,
In pagentes set fourth apparently to all eyne
The olde and newe testament, with livelye comforth,
Interminglinge therewith, onely to make sporte,
Some thinges not warranted by any writt,
Which to gladd the hearers he woulde men to take yt.

.　　.　　.　　.　　.　　.　　.

As in this citie divers yeares the have bene set out,
Soe at this tyme of Pentecoste; called Whitsontyde,
Allthough to all the citie followe labour and coste,
Yet God giving leave that tyme shall you, in playe,
For three dayes together, begyninge on Mondaye,
See these pagentes played to the beste of theire skill ;
When to supplye all wants shalbe noé wantes of good will.

.　　.　　.　　.　　.　　.　　.

This worthy Knighte, Arnway, then mayor of this citie,
This order toke, as declare to you I shall,
That by 24 occupations, artes, craftes, or misterie,
These pagentes should be played, after breefe rehearsall ;
For everye pagente a carriage to be provyded withall ;
In which sorte we porpose, this Whitsontyde,
Our pageantes into three partes to devyde."

The remaining verses indicate the subject of the play to be enacted on each pageant, and the guild or craft by which it will be played. Thus—

" The appearinge angell and starr upon Christes birth,
To sheapeardes poore, of base and lowe degree,
You Painters and Glasiors decke out with all meirthe,
And see that Gloria in excelsis be songe merelye."

When the heralds have done, the pageants are at length permitted to start upon their long round. They are drawn by men or by horses. In the former case it is the privilege of the journeymen of the craft, who are not engaged as actors, to fill the place of draught horses. In 1433, the Weaver's Company of Coventry passed the following resolution :—" Also it is ordeyned that the journeymen of the said

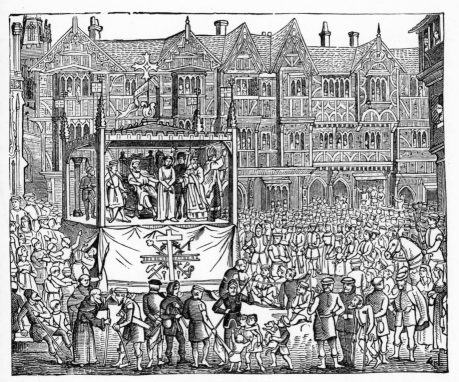

A MYSTERY PLAY.

craft schall have yearly six shillings and eight pence, and for that they schall have owte the paggent, and on Corpus Christi day to dryve it from place to place ther as it schal be played, and then for to brynge it geyn into the paggent-house, without any hurte, nyther defawte, and they for to put the master to no more coste." The Smiths of Coventry, in 1490, paid one shilling and twopence for having their pageant moved from place to place ; while at York, in 1584, it took six labourers to drag the Baker's pageant, for which they received two shillings. The Coventry Drapers and Cappers employed respectively ten and twelve men for the same purpose.

It cannot have been easy work to move these heavy vehicles about the ill-paved streets of our old cities, and a striking testimony to either the clumsiness of the pageants or the badness of the roads is afforded by the frequent entries in the Companies' accounts of such items as, " for sope for the pagent wheles," " talowe to the pagent," " paid for shope and gresse to the wheles." Horses, however, were often harnessed to the cars, and the accounts show many payments for the hire of animals and harness, and for providing the drivers with meat and drink. The Coventry Cappers were probably wise in their generation when they hired a carpenter to accompany their pageant, so that any mishap could at once be attended to.

The pageants were either escorted through the city by a guard of craftsmen, or men were hired to stand round it, and to keep order among the audiences. In 1476, the Company of Armourers, at York, ordered " that all the masters of the same craft from now forth yearly, on Corpus Christi day, in the morning, be ready in their own proper

5

persons, every one of them with an honest weapon, to await upon their pageant-masters and pageant, at the playing and setting forth their said pageant, at the first place where they shall begin. And so to await upon the same their pageant through the city, to the play be played as of that same pageant." And in 1493 the Spurriers and Lorimers made a similar regulation.

The pageants were drawn from street to street, and station to station, in proper order. Archdeacon Rogers, who saw the plays acted at Chester, in 1594, has described the mode of exhibition :—

> " The maner of these playes were, every company had his pagiant, which pagiants weare a high scafold with two roumes, a higher and a lower, upon four wheels. In the lower they apparelled themselves, and in the higher roume they played, beinge all open on the tope, that all behoulders might heare and see them. The places where they played them was in every streete. They began first at the Abay gates, and when the first pagiante was played it was wheeled to the highe crosse before the Mayor, and so to every streete, and soe every streete had a pagiant playing before them at one time, till all the pagiantes for the day appointed weare playen, and when one pagiant was neere ended, worde was broughte from streete to streete, that soe they might come in place thereof, exceedinge orderlye, and all the streetes have their pagiantes afore them all at one time playeinge together ; to see w'ch playes was greate resorte, and also scafoldes and stages made in the streetes in those places where they determined to playe their pagiantes."

Dugdale, in his "Antiquities of Warwickshire," gives similar information about the Coventry pageants. He says, that there they "had theaters for the severall scenes very large and high, placed upon wheels, and drawn to all the eminent parts of the city, for the better advantage of spectators." By this arrangement, a complete succession of plays was kept up throughout the city from dawn to dusk, a

plan which prevented undue crowding at any one point, a
very desirable thing in those days of narrow streets, and gave
everyone an opportunity of witnessing the entire series of plays.

The actors were paid for their services, the rate of
remuneration depending on the length, not the dignity, of
the parts.   So far as we can learn, Pilate was the most highly
paid character—his representative at Coventry in 1490
received 4s., Herod and Caiaphas ranking next with 3s. 4d.
each, while the actor who played God or Jesus, surely a most
trying rôle, seeing that the play dealt with the Trial and
Passion, had to be content with 2s., the same sum being
paid to Pilate's wife.   Here are some other entries in the
salary list for that year :—

> " Itm to the Bedull, iiijd.
> Itm to one of the Knights, ijs.
> Itm to the devyll and to Judas, xviijd.
> Itm to Peter and to Malchus, xvjd.
> Itm to Anna, ijs., ijd.
> Itm to Pilatte is sonne, iiijd.
> Itm to another Knighte, ijs."

At Hull, wages ruled low at first, but gradually rose by
increments of a few pence at a time.   In 1447, God received
6d., in 1484, 8d., in 1487, 10d., and in 1520 his salary
reached the maximum of one shilling.   In 1485, Noah got
8d., and his wife 1s., which sums were increased in 1520 to
2s. and 1s. 6d. respectively.   Sometimes an actor undertook
to play two characters, and then his remuneration seems to
have been slightly increased.   In the accounts of the
Coventry Smiths, for 1584, are some items of payments for
doubling parts :—

> " Itm payd to Reignolde Headly for playinge of Symon and
> Phynea, vs.

Itm payd to John Hoppers for playing of Jesus and Zacharyas, iijs.

Itm payd to John Green for playinge of Matthias and Esron, ijs."

The general utility man existed in those days, and seems to have been, in comparison with the leading actors, fairly well paid. Thus at Coventry a man named Fawston got 4d. for hanging Judas, 4d. for cock-crowing, and 5d. for setting the world on fire in the last scene of all.

Besides their wages, the actors received liberal rations of food and ale. Pilate, as the leading man, was permitted to drink wine, in order, perhaps, to mark his superiority to the common run of actors, who were obliged to content themselves with home-brewed beer. Judging from the charges made by the pageant-masters against their Guilds, the progress of the pageants must have been frequently interrupted in order that the players and all concerned might eat and drink. We are told that they refreshed themselves "at every reste." Before the plays commenced a breakfast was provided ; dinner was served at mid-day, roast beef and goose finding places on the board ; and after the day's labours were over, all partook of a hearty supper. This last meal cost the Coventry Smiths, in 1584, the sum of eight shillings and sixpence, and we can form some idea of the magnitude of the meal, when we recollect that a rib of beef or a goose could be purchased for about 3d. or 4d., and that ale was 2d. a gallon. Such entries as the following occur over and over again in the various accounts :—Drink to players, ijs. ; drivers for drink, iiijd. ; spent at tavern, xijd. ; drink to musicians, ijd. ; drink at the pageant, viijd. ; item for ix gallons of ale, xviijd. ; for a quarte of wyne, ijd.

We have hitherto spoken of the guilds as each producing their own plays, but this was not always done, for sometimes a guild, or a number of guilds, would contract with a person skilled in the stage craft of the day to produce their play or plays for them. In 1452, by an agreement made on the Monday before Palm Sunday, the Smiths' Company of Coventry agreed with one, Thoms Colclow, that he should produce their pageant for the next twelve years. The text of the agreement has been preserved, and runs as follows :—
" That Thoms Colclow, skinner, ffro this day forth shall have the rewle of the pajaunt unto the end of twelve years next following. He for to find the players, and all that longeth thereto all the seide time, save the kep of the craft shall let bring forth the pajant, and find clothes that gon about the pajant, and find rushes thereto ; and every Whit-sun week who that be keps of the craft shall dine with Colclow, and every master lay down fourpence, and Colclow shall have yearly for his labour forty-six shillings and eight-pence, and he to bring into the master on Sunday next after Corpus Christi day the original (that is, the play-book), and fetch his seven nobles ; and Colclow must bring in at the latter end of the time all the garments that longen to the pajant as good as they were delivered to him." In 1591, all the Coventry Companies contracted with a man named Massye for the production of their plays.

CHAPTER IX.

The Scenery, Properties and Dresses.

THE limited stage-room at the disposal of the producers of a miracle play in England precluded any very ambitious attempts in the way of scenery, indeed moveable scenes, as we understand them, were unknown in this country until after the Restoration. Still something was done to give an appropriate, or what was considered to be an appropriate appearance to the pageants on which the various plays were enacted. For instance, in the play of the Creation painted cloths were, probably, unrolled at the proper time to pictorially illustrate the action of the Creator. In a French Mystery of 1542 we find that at the separation of light from darkness they displayed a cloth, one half of which was coloured white and the other half black. When fish were made, the stage direction was, "show a sea with fish in the sea;" and, similarly, at the creation of the heavenly bodies, "Show a sky painted all over with stars and the names of planets." The direction for the creation of birds was very naïve—"Then one ought in secret to put little birds flying in the air and alighting upon the earth, with the most foreign birds that one is able to procure." It is perhaps not going too far to assume that if these primitive methods were used in the neighbouring country of France, something of the same kind was to be seen on the English pageants, although the necessity of leaving the stage open to the audience on at least three sides would prevent any extensive user of anything likely to obstruct the view.

In the play of the Flood we know that a large "practical" Ark was used, and in those plays where part of the action was supposed to take place within a house, and part in the open country or in a street, a building of some sort would be erected at the back or side of the stage, with an open front, so that the audience could see what was passing inside. The stable at Bethlehem, and the hut in the Wakefield Shepherds' Play, will at once occur to the reader as instances. Other erections of this kind, which Halliwell-Phillips has aptly described as not unlike "decorated sentry boxes," would represent the Palaces of Herod and Pilate, the Temple at Jerusalem, the room in which the Last Supper was eaten, the Synagogue, and so on.   For other plays tapestries were hung round the pageant, on which various incidents of the play were painted.   Thus we find in the inventories of the possessions of the guilds such items as "halfe a yarde of Rede Sea," "three paynted clothes to hang abowte the pageant," and "two pajiont clothes of the Passion."

In many of the plays two pageants or stages were required, as well as some smaller scaffolds or stages which were appropriated to the use of individual characters.   Such a play was the Trial of Christ, where Herod, Pilate, and the High Priest each had their separate stage, the actors going from one stage to the other as the action required. Another, and perhaps a better example, is furnished by the plays of the Council of the Jews and the Last Supper in the Coventry series.   These plays were probably represented together, and the texts contain some very quaint stage directions, which well show the primitive nature of the scenic arrangements, and also give minute particulars of the costumes to be worn by the characters.   In the Council of the Jews, Annas and Caiaphas each has his stage, which is supposed to represent his house, and between the two is a third stage, which is the Council House.   We are first introduced to Annas—"Here xal Annas shewyn hymself in his stage be seyn after a busshop of the hoold lawe, in a skarlet gowne, and over that a blew tabbard furryd with whyte, and a mytere on his hed, after the hoold lawe; ij doctorys stondyng by him in furryd hodys, and on (one) beforn hem with his staff of astat, and eche of hem on here hedys a furryd cappe, with a gret knop in the crowne, and on stondyng beforn as a Sarazyn, the wiche xal be his masangere."

Annas wishes to discuss with Caiaphas the action they are to take respecting Jesus, so he sends his messenger or Saracen to invite him to a conference.   The messenger leaves the scaffold and makes his way to the stage representing the house of Caiaphas.

"In the meantime (I modernise the spelling), Caiaphas shews himself in his scaffold, arrayed like to Annas, saving his tabard shall be red, furred with white; two doctors with him arrayed with pellises after the old guise, and furred caps on their heads."

The messenger salutes the High Priest and tells his business, Caiaphas expresses his readiness to meet Annas, and sends the messenger back to say so.   Then the two dignitaries leave their scaffolds and ascend the centre stage with their servants and the Pharisees.   This "myd place" is arranged to represent "a lytil oratory, with stolys and cusshonys clenly beseyn, lyche as it were a cownsel-hous."

By-and-bye, the twenty-sixth pageant arrives, and on it is set forth the triumphal entry of Christ into Jerusalem, and then comes the twenty-seventh of the series, the scene of which is the exterior and interior of Symon's house.

" Here Cryst enteryth into the hous with his disciplis and ete the Paschal lomb ; and in the mene tyme the cownsel-hous befornseyd xal sodeynly onclose, schewyng the bus-chopps, prestys, and jewgys syttyng in here astat, lyke as it were a convocacyon."

This sudden unclosing was nothing more than the drawing apart of the curtains that had been hung across the front of the meeting-place of the Jews, for which purpose certain of the pageants were provided with curtain hooks and rings.

Soon Judas slips away from Symon's house, and crosses over to the Council house, where he arranges to betray his Master.   The High Priests and their followers then separate, and go back to their own scaffolds, while the room in Symon's house in turn " suddenly uncloses," and shows Christ and his disciples partaking of the Last Supper. Such were the simple devices by which the old actors made the story they had to tell clear to their uncritical and friendly audiences.

If their scenery was primitive, their properties were beyond reproach.   Their crosses, spears, tools, and such like, were as realistic as wood and paint could well be.   The old property masters had a passion for gilt, they gilded every-thing they could ; the cross, the post to which Jesus was tied when he was scourged, the hair of God's wig, his throne, and even his face, till they learned by experience the dangers of the practice.   They made horses and other beasts of

hoops and canvas, artificial clouds, trees, tombs, and beds.
Storm, lightning, thunder, and rain were ready at hand, and
they even managed an earthquake, with the aid of a huge
barrel filled with stones, which they kept in the room below
the stage, in company with windlasses for raising angels aloft,
and other strange contrivances.   Globes of some combustible
substance were contrived to represent this world of ours,
and were duly set on fire and consumed when the Day of
Judgment was played.

> " Payd for the baryll for the yerthequake ; payd for tyntyng
> (attending) the yerthequake, iiij.d. ; payd for starche to make
> the storm, vj.d. ; payd for makyng of iij worldys, ijs.; payd
> for pantyng of the worldys ; payd for settynge the world of
> fyer, v.d. ; payd for kepyng the wynd, vj.d."

are a few of the entries in the old account books.

But the masterpiece of realism was Hell Mouth, perhaps
the most popular and most eagerly awaited feature of the
Miracle plays.   In any play in which the Devil took part
Hell Mouth was sure to figure, though it was in plays like
the Harrowing of Hell and Doomesday that it attained its
greatest magnificence.   It was generally represented as a
square, embattled tower, the entrance to which was through
a gaping and hideous dragon's head, with glaring eyes,
enormous nose, and moveable jaws lined with rows of long,
projecting teeth.

> " An hideous hole all vaste, withouten shape,
>   Of endlesse depth, orewhelm'd with ragged stone,
> With ougly mouth, and griesly jawes doth gape,
>   And to our sight confounds itself in one."

When the jaws opened, fire and smoke, produced by
braziers and bellows hidden away behind, were vomited
from the mouth and nostrils.   Drums were beaten, horns

HELL MOUTH.
(From an Old German Print.)

blown, tin-cans banged, and amid the wild din the devil and his imps leapt in and out of the flaming opening, to drag the wicked characters to limbo, or to stir up the unhappy occupants of the infernal regions.

To have a good Hell Mouth was the great and absorbing ambition of the old stage managers, and many are the entries relating to it—

> Item, paide ior payntyng and makyng new hell hede, xij.d.
> Item, payd for mendyng new hell hede, vj.d.
> P'd to Jhon Huyt for payntyng of hell mowthe, xvj.d.
> P'd for makyng hell mouth and cloth for hyt, iiij.s.
> Payde for kepynge hell hede, viij.d.
> Item, payd for kepyng of fyer at hell mothe, iiij.d.

The costumes worn by the various characters were both curious and costly. Saints and holy persons were distinguished by gilt hair and beards. Christ wore a long sheepskin. Herod was dressed as a Saracen, and bore a formidable looking sword. He was represented as always being in a passion, and was sometimes attended by a small boy, armed with a bladder tied to a stick, whose duty was to beat Herod whenever his rage gave signs of abating, and so stir him up to fresh fury. The Shakesperean expression " to out—Herod Herod," indicates the extravagance with which the part was played. Demons wore hideous masks, as they still do in pantomimes, and angels were made supremely happy, and, we must think, uncomfortable, by having to wear gilded skins, and golden wings fastened to their shoulders. They also wore flowing white surplices, and had diadems on their heads. The Devil was a very prominent character, for he wore horns and a tail, and a bright red beard. His coat and hose were made of rough hair, and he was intended to present an uncouth and horrible appearance. Both he and

Pilate carried huge clubs made of leather and stuffed with wool. The First Person in the Trinity was represented as a pope, with a tiara and sceptre, while the leaders of the Jews were attired as bishops in mitres, hoods, and rochets. Adam and Eve in the garden of Eden were dressed in close-fitting coats of white leather and hose, stained or dyed to (probably) a flesh colour. At the proper time they put on, over these "fleshings," rough garments of skins.

> " Two cotes and a payre hosen for Eve stayned ; a cote and hosen for Adam steyned."

The tradition that they appeared naked on the stage is quite unfounded, and it is hardly necessary to say that the female characters were acted by men or boys. Most of the characters wore gloves, and those who did not conceal their features behind masks had their faces painted.

> Item paid for gloves to the pleyares, xixd.
> Item paid for a pair of gloves for God.
> Item paid to the peynter for peynting of ther ffases, viijd.
> Item paid for pyntyng off ther fasus, ijd.

Finally, the lost souls wore parti-coloured dresses of black and yellow to represent flames, and they had their faces blackened.

Miracle plays ceased to be acted in this country about the year 1600, by which time our unequalled English drama had almost reached the summit of its glory. Shakespeare, Marlowe, Jonson, Beaumont, Fletcher, Massenger, Webster, and others, were busily building up that great mass of dramatic literature, which is the pride of Englishmen and the envy of the civilized world. Almost at one bound, England leapt from the tied-down conventionality of the miracle play to a drama abounding in life and energy. I do not claim for the miracle play that it exerted any very great influence on our subsequent drama, but this may be said for it, it certainly made Shakespeare possible.   It had fostered a national love of acting ; it had taught men to exercise their imaginations, and to "make-believe ;" it had made drama the popular amusement.   It had sown the seed of comedy, and had already marked out the broad distinctions between historical plays, comedies, and tragedies ; and, greatest result of all, it had for ever knocked on the head, so far as English drama is concerned, the great fallacy of classic drama, that tragedy and comedy were and must be distinct rituals ; in other words it promulgated the great canon of Romantic art, that tragedy on the stage is made more effective and more impressive when the serious and painful episodes are separated and relieved by the introduction of pleasing and humorous incidents and characters ; that as tragedy and comedy clash and mingle in our daily life, so they must go hand in hand to make a perfect play, which is, or should be, but a picture of more or less idealised life.

Appendix.

──────⟨◆⟩──────

I.—THE ORDER OF THE YORK PLAYS.

"THE order of the Pageants of the Play of Corpus Christi, in the time of the mayoralty of William Alne, in the third year of the reign of King Henry the Fifth, after the Conquest of England, compiled by Roger Burton, town clerk, in the year 1415." (Translation).

PERFORMED BY.	SUBJECT AND CHARACTERS.
1. TANNERS.	God the Father Almighty creating and forming the heavens, angels, and archangels, Lucifer and the angels that fell with him to hell.
2. PLASTERERS.	God the Father in his own substance creating the earth and all which is therein, by the space of five days.
3. CARDMAKERS [*i.e.*, the makers of cards for combing wool].	God the Father creating Adam of the clay of the earth, and making Eve of Adam's rib, and inspiring them with the breath of life.
4. FULLERS.	God forbidding Adam and Eve to eat of the tree of life.
5. COOPERS.	Adam and Eve and a tree betwixt them ; the serpent deceiving them with apples ; God speaking to them and cursing the serpent, and with a sword driving them out of Paradise.

6. ARMOURERS.	Adam and Eve, an angel with a spade and distaff assigning them work.
7. GAUNTERS or GLOVERS.	Abel and Cain offering victims in sacrifice.
8. SHIPWRIGHTS.	God warning Noah to make an Ark of floatable wood.
9. PESSONERS (Fishmongers) and MARINERS.	Noah in the Ark, with his wife; the three sons of Noah with their wives; with divers animals.
10. PARCHMENT-MAKERS and BOOKBINDERS.	Abraham sacrificing his son Isaac on an altar, a boy with wood, and an angel.
11. HOSIERS.	Moses lifting up the serpent in the wilderness; King Pharaoh; eight Jews wondering and expecting.
12. SPICERS or GROCERS.	A doctor declaring the sayings of the prophets of the future birth of Christ. Mary; an angel saluting her; Mary saluting Elizabeth.
13. PEWTERERS and FOUNDERS [*i.e.* the metal melters and moulders].	Mary, Joseph. wishing to put her away; an angel speaking to them that they go to Bethlehem.
14. TYLERS [*i.e.* thatchers].	Mary, Joseph, a midwife; the Child born, lying in a manger betwixt an ox and an ass, and an angel speaking to the shepherds, and to the players in the next pageant.
15. CHANDLERS.	The shepherds talking together, the star in the East; an angel giving the shepherds the good tidings of the Child's birth.

16. ORFEVERS or GOLD-
17. SMITHS, GOLDBEATERS
and MONEYMAKERS.

The three Kings coming from the East, Herod asking them about the child Jesus; the son of Herod, two counsellors, and a messenger. Mary with the Child, a star above, and the three Kings offering gifts.

41. HATMAKERS, MASONS, and LABOURERS.

Mary with the Child, Joseph, Anna, the midwife with young pigeons; Simeon receiving the Child in his arms, and two sons of Simeon.

[This play, though numbered 41 in Burton's list, is obviously misplaced, and should come between the plays he numbers 17 and 18. The play was at one time performed by the Brothers of the Hospital of St. Leonard.]

18. MARSSHALS [*i.e.* the shoers of horses and Veterinaries].

Mary with the Child, and Joseph fleeing into Egypt at the bidding of an angel.

19. GIRDLERS, NAILERS, and SAWYERS.

Herod commanding the children to be slain; four soldiers with lances; two counsellors of the King, and four women lamenting the slaughter of the children.

20. SPURRIERS and LORIMERS (bit-makers).

The Doctors, the Child Jesus sitting in the Temple in their midst, questioning and answering them. Four Jews, Mary and Joseph seeking Him, and finding Him in the Temple.

21. BARBERS.

Jesus, John the Baptist baptizing Him.

[21A]. VINTNERS.

Jesus, Mary, bridegroom with bride, the Ruler of the Feast with his household, with six water-pots, in which the water is turned into wine.

6

22. FEWERS or SMITHS.   Jesus upon the pinnacle of the
                               Temple, Satan tempting Him,
                               with stones, and two angels
                               ministering.

23. CURRIERS.   Peter, James, and John; Jesus
                               ascending into the mountain
                               and transfiguring Himself before
                               them; Moses and Elias appear-
                               ing, and a voice speaking from a
                               cloud.

[23A]. IRONMONGERS.   Jesus, and Simon the Leper
                               asking Jesus to eat with him;
                               two disciples, Mary Magdalene
                               washing the feet of Jesus with
                               her tears, and wiping them with
                               her hair.

24. PLUMBERS and   Jesus, two Apostles, the woman
    PATTEN-MAKERS.   taken in adultery, four Jews
                               accusing her.

[24A]. POUCH-MAKERS,   Lazarus in the tomb, Mary
    BOTTELLERS, and   Magdalene, Martha, and two
    CAP-MAKERS.   Jews in wonderment.

25. SKINNERS.   Jesus upon an ass with its foal,
                               xii. Apostles following Jesus, six
                               rich and six poor men, eight boys
                               with branches of palms, singing
                               Benedictus, etc., and Zacchaeus
                               climbing into a sycamore tree.

26. CUTLERS, BLADE-
    SMITHS, SHEATHERS,   Pilate, Caiaphas, two soldiers,
    SCALERS, BUCKLE-   three Jews, Judas selling Jesus.
    MAKERS, and HORNERS.

27. BAXTERS or BAKERS.   The paschal lamb, the Lord's
                               Supper, the xii. Apostles, Jesus
                               girt with a linen towel washing
                               their feet; the institution of the
                               Sacrament of Christ's Body in
                               the New Law; the communion
                               of the Apostles.

28. CORDWANERS or Shoemakers.

Pilate, Caiaphas, Annas, fourteen armed soldiers, Malchus, Peter, James, John, Jesus, and Judas kissing and betraying Him.

29. BOWERS and FLETCHERS (Arrow-featherers).

Jesus, Annas, Caiaphas, and four Jews persecuting and scourging Jesus. Peter, the woman accusing Peter, and Malchus.

30. TAPISERS and COUCHERS [*i.e.*, Tapestry-weavers and Couch-coverers].

Jesus, Pilate, Annas, Caiaphas, two counsellors, and four Jews accusing Christ.

31. LITTESTERS [*i.e.*, Bedmakers].

Herod, two counsellors, four soldiers, Jesus, and three Jews.

32. COOKS and WATER-LEADERS.

Pilate, Annas, Caiaphas, two Jews, and Judas bringing back to them the thirty pieces of silver.

[32A]. SALSE-MAKERS or Sauce-makers.

The Hanging of Judas.

[This play is not in Burton's list.]

33. TILEMAKERS, MILLERS, ROPERS, SIEVERS, TURNERS, HAYRESTERS (Workers in horse-hair), and BOLLERS (bowl-makers).

Jesus, Pilate, Caiaphas, Annas, six soldiers carrying spears and ensigns, and four others leading Jesus from Herod, desiring Barabbas to be released and Jesus to be crucified, and then binding and scourging Him, placing a crown of thorns upon His head ; three soldiers casting lots for the vest of Jesus.

34. TUNNERS or SHERMEN [*i.e.*, those who cut the nap off cloth].

Jesus, covered with blood, bearing His Cross to Calvary ; Simon of Cyrene, Jews compelling him to bear the Cross ; Mary, the mother of Jesus, the Apostle John informing her of the condemnation of her Son, and of His journey to Calvary ; Veronica wiping blood and sweat from the face of Jesus with the napkin on which is imprinted Jesus's face; and other women lamenting Jesus.

35. PINNERS or wire-workers, LATONERS, and PAINTERS.

The Cross, Jesus stretched upon it on the earth, four Jews scourging and dragging Him with ropes, and afterwards uplifting the Cross, and the body of Jesus nailed to it, on Mount Calvary.

36. BUTCHERS and POULTERERS.

The Cross, two thieves cruci-fied, Jesus hung on the Cross between them, Mary the mother of Jesus, John, Mary, James, and Salome. Longeus with a lance, a slave with a sponge, Pilate, Annas, Caiaphas, a centurion, Joseph of Arimathea and Nico-demus laying Him in the tomb.

37. SELLERS or Sadlers, VERROURS or Glaziers, and FUYSTOURS [those who made saddle-trees].

Jesus despoiling Hell, twelve spirits, six good and six bad.

38. CARPENTERS.

Jesus rising from the tomb, four soldiers armed, and the three Maries lamenting. Pilate, Caia-phas.

NOTE.—When the soldiers inform Pilate that Christ has risen, they are told to tell the people that He was taken away by twenty thousand armed men. For consenting to spread this falsehood, they are given a thousand pounds and promised promotion. Pilate moralises :—

" Thus schall the sothe be bought and solde,
And treasonne schall for trewthe be tolde."

39. WINEDRAWERS

Jesus, Mary Magdalene with spices.

40. BROGGOURS [*i.e.* Brokers] and WOOL-PACKERS. [The SLEDGEMEN or Carriers also performed this play].

Jesus, Luke and Cleophas in the guise of Pilgrims.

41. [See above, between Nos. 17 and 18.]

42. SCRIVENERS, LUMINERS [*i.e.* Illuminators], QUES-TORS [*i.e.* Pardoners] and DUBBERS [*i.e.* the cloth furbishers.]

Jesus, Peter, John, James and other apostles. Thomas feeling the wounds of Jesus.

43. TALLIAUNDERS [*i.e.* Tailors.]

Mary, John the Evangelist, two Angels, and eleven Apostles ; Jesus ascending before them, and four angels carrying a cloud.

44. POTTERS.

Mary, two Angels, eleven Apostles, and the Holy Spirit descending on them, and four Jews in wonderment.

45. DRAPERS.

Jesus, Mary, Gabriel with two Angels, two virgins, and three Jews of the kindred of Mary, eight Apostles and two Devils.

[45A]. LINEN-WEAVERS.

A play, omitted in the MS., called Fergus, and founded on an incident in the apocryphal legend of the Death of the Virgin Mary.

46. WOOLLEN-WEAVERS.

Mary ascending with a crowd of Angels, eight apostles, and Thomas, the Apostle, preaching in the desert.

47. HOSTILERS or INN-KEEPERS.

Mary, Jesus crowning her, singing with a crowd of Angels.

40. MERCERS.

Jesus, Mary, twelve Apostles, four angels with trumpets, and four with a crown, a lance and two scourges ; four good spirits and four evil spirits, and six devils.

II.—Extract from City Register of York relating to the Performance of the Miracle Plays in 1426 (translated).

"In the name of God. Amen. Whereas for a long course of time the articifiers and tradesmen of the city of York have, at their own expense, acted plays; and particularly a certain sumptuous play, exhibited in several pageants, wherein the history of the Old and New Testament in divers places of the said city, in the feast of Corpus Christi, by a solemn procession is represented, in reverence to the sacrament of the body of Christ. Beginning first at the great gates of the priory of the Holy Trinity in York, and so going in procession to and into the Cathedral Church of the same; and afterwards to the hospital of St. Leonard, in York, leaving the aforesaid sacrament in that place. Preceded by a vast number of lighted torches, and a great multitude of priests in their proper habits, and followed by the mayor and citizens, with a prodigious crowd of the populace attending.

"And whereas, upon this, a certain very religious father, William Melton, of the order of the Friars Minors, professor of holy pageantry (?) and a most famous preacher of the word of God, coming to this city, in several sermons recommended the aforesaid play to the people, affirming that it was good in itself, and very commendable so to do. Yet also said that the citizens of the said city, and other strangers coming to the said feast, had greatly disgraced the play by revellings, drunkenness, shouts, songs, and other insolencies, little regarding the divine offices of the said day. And what is to be lamented they lose, for that reason, the Indulgences by the holy father, Pope Urban IV. (who instituted the Feast of Corpus Christi in 1264), in this part graciously conceded. Those, namely, faithful in Christ, who attended (here follow the indulgences), and therefore, as it seemed most wholesome to the said father William, the people of the city were inclined that the play should be played on one day, and the procession on another, so that the people might attend divine service at the churches on the said feast for the indulgences aforesaid.

"WHEREFORE Peter Buckey, mayor of this city of York (here follow names of two Sheriffs, ten Alderman, and twenty-one burgesses), were met in the Council Chamber of the said city, the 6th day of June, 1426, and by the said wholesome exhortations and admonitions of the said father William being incited, that it is no crime, nor can it offend God, if good be converted into better.

"THEREFORE, having diligently considered of the premises, they gave their express and unanimous consent that the course aforesaid should be published to. the whole city in the Common Hall of the same, and having their consent that the premises should be better reformed. Upon which the aforesaid mayor convened the citizens together in the said hall, the 10th day of the month aforesaid and the same year, and made proclamation in a solemn manner, where it was ordained by the common assent that this solemn play of Corpus Christi should be played every year on the vigil of the said feast, and that the procession should be made constantly on the day of the said feast, so that all people being in the said city might have leisure to attend devoutly the matins, vespers, and the other hours of the said feast, and be made partakers of the indulgences in that part by the said Roman Pope Urban the fourth most graciously granted and confirmed."

III.—THE ORDER OF THE WAKEFIELD PLAYS.

1. The Creation of the World, and of Adam and Eve. The Fall.
2. Cain and Abel.
3. The Building of the Ark, and the Flood.
4. The Sacrifice of Isaac.
5. Jacob and Esau.
6. Processus Prophetarum.
7. Israel in Egypt.
8. Cæsar Augustus orders the World to be taxed.
9. The Annunciation.
10. The Salutation.
11. The First and Second Shepherd's Plays.
12. The Visit of the Wise Men of the East.

13. The Flight into Egypt.
14. The Massacre of the Innocents.
15. The Purification.
16. Jesus in the Temple.
17. John the Baptist.
18. The Last Supper, and the Betrayal.
19. The Trial before Caiaphas.
20. The Trial before Pilate.
21. The Crucifixion.
22. Processus Talentorum.
23. The Harrowing of Hell.
24. The Resurrection.
25. The Appearance of Christ on the Road to Emaus.
26. The Appearance to Thomas.
27. The Ascension.
28. The Day of Judgment.
29. The Raising of Lazarus. [This play is obviously misplaced].
30. The Hanging of Judas. [Added to the MS. about the sixteenth century].

IV.—THE ORDER OF THE CHESTER PLAYS.

PERFORMED BY.	SUBJECT.
1. TANNERS.	The Fall of Lucifer.
2. DRAPERS.	The Creation of the World, Adam and Eve, and how Cain slew Abel.
3. WATER-DRAWERS.	The Ark, and the Flood.
4. BARBERS and WAX CHANDLERS.	The Histories of Lot and Abraham, the sacrifice of Isaac, and the offering of Melchizedek.
5. CAPPERS and LINEN-DRAPERS.	Story of Balaam and Balak.
6. WRIGHTS and SLATERS.	The Birth of Christ.
7. PAINTERS and GLAZIERS.	The Shepherd's Play.
8. VINTNERS.	The Visit of the three Kings, and Processus Prophetarum.

9. MERCERS.	The offerings of the three Kings, and their return to their own countries.
10. GOLDSMITHS and MASONS.	The Massacre of the Innocents.
11. SMITHS.	Christ in the Temple.
12. BUTCHERS.	The Temptation in the Wilderness.
13. GLOVERS.	The Raising of Lazarus, and the healing of Cecus, the blind man.
14. CORVISORS.	The Journey of Our Saviour to Jerusalem.
15. BAKERS.	The Last Supper.
16. FLESHERS, BOWYERS, COOPERS, STRINGERS, and IRONMONGERS.	The Passion and Crucifixion.
17. COOKS.	The Harrowing of Hell.
18. SKINNERS.	The Resurrection.
19. SADLERS and FFUST-ERERS [saddle-tree makers.]	The Appearances of Christ after His Resurrection.
20. TAILORS.	The Ascension.
21. FISHMONGERS.	The Descent of the Holy Spirit.
22. SHERMEN.	A play dealing with the prophecies of the coming of Anti-Christ.
23.	A play in which the Old Testament prophecies are explained.
24. DVERS and HEWSTERS.	Anti-Christ.
25. WEAVERS.	The Last Judgment.

V.—THE ORDER OF THE GREY FRIARS' PLAYS AT COVENTRY.

1. The Creation.
2. The Temptation and Fall.
3. Cain and Abel.
4. The Flood.
5. Abraham and Isaac.
6. Moses and the Tables of the Law.   (A monologue by Moses.)
7. The Prophecies relating to Christ.
8. The Barrenness of Anna.
9. Mary in the Temple.
10. The Betrothal of Mary and Joseph.
11. The Salutation and Conception.
12. The Return of Joseph.
13. The Visit to Elizabeth.
14. The Trial of Joseph and Mary.   (In this play we have a trial by ordeal illustrated).
15. The Birth of Christ.
16. The Adoration by the Shepherds.
17. The Visit of the Magi.
18. The Purification.
19. The Massacre of the Innocents, and the Rejoicing and Death of Herod.   (Herod and his knights are represented as feasting after the slaughter of the children.   Death appears, and carries off Herod, and hands him over to the tender mercies of the Devil).
20. Christ in the Temple among the Doctors.
21. The Baptism of Christ.
22. The Temptation in the Wilderness.
23. The Woman taken in Adultery.
24. The Raising of Lazarus.
25. The Council of the Jews.
26. Christ's Entry into Jerusalem.
27. The Last Supper.
28. The Passion and betrayal.
29.
30. } The Trials of Christ.   (Probably performed together).
31. The Dream of Pilate's Wife.
32. The Condemnation and Crucifixion.

33. The Harrowing of Hell.
34. The Burial of Jesus.
35. The Resurrection.
36. The Three Maries at the Tomb.
37. The Appearance to Mary Magdalene.
38. The Appearance on the road to Emaus.
39. The Ascension.
40. The Descent of the Holy Spirit.
41. The Assumption of Mary.
42. The Last Judgment.

VI.—ADVERTISEMENT OF A MIRACLE PLAY PERFORMED IN A PUPPET SHOW AT BARTHOLOMEW FAIR, EARLY IN THE EIGHTEENTH CENTURY.

"By Her Majestie's permission. At Hartley's booth over against the Cross and Daggers, next to Mr. Miller's booth, during the time of Bartholomew Fair will be presented a little opera, called THE OLD CREATION OF THE WORLD, newly reviv'd, with the addition of the glorious battle obtained over the French and Spaniards by his Grace the Duke of Marlborough.

"The contents are these :—

1. The Creation of Adam and Eve.
2. The intreagues of Lucifer in the Garden of Eden.
3. Adam and Eve driven out of Paradise.
4. Cain going to plow, Abel driving sheep.
5. Cain killeth his brother Abel.
6. Abraham offering his son Isaac.
7. Three Wise men of the East guided by a star, who worship Him.
8. Joseph and Mary flew (*sic*) away by night upon an ass.
9. King Herod's cruelty; his men's spears laden with children.
10. Rich Dives invites his friends, and orders his porter to keep the beggers from his gate.
11. Poor Lazarus comes a-begging at rich Dives's gate, and the dogs lick his sores.
12. The Good Angel and Death contend for Lazarus's life.

13. Rich Dives taken sick and dieth. He is buried in great solemnity.

14. Rich Dives in Hell and Lazarus in Abraham's bosom, seen in a most glorious object, all in machines descending in a throne, guarded with multitudes of Angels, with the breaking of the clouds, discovering the Palace of the Sun, in double and treble prospects, to the admiration of all spectators. Likewise several rich and large figures, with dances, jiggs, sarabands, anticks, and country dances between every Act; compleated with the merry humours of John Spendall and Punchanello, with several other things never yet exposed.

Performed by Mat. Heatly.

Vivat Regina!"

Index.